OECD *Economic Surveys* Electronic Books

The OECD, recognising the strategic role of electronic publishing, will be issuing the OECD *Economic Surveys*, both for the Member countries and for countries of Central and Eastern Europe covered by the Organisation's Centre for Co-operation with Economies in Transition, as electronic books with effect from the 1994/1995 series -- incorporating the text, tables and figures of the printed version. The information will appear on screen in an identical format, including the use of colour in graphs.

The electronic book, which retains the quality and readability of the printed version throughout, will enable readers to take advantage of the new tools that the ACROBAT software (included on the diskette) provides by offering the following benefits:

- ❑ User-friendly and intuitive interface
- ❑ Comprehensive index for rapid text retrieval, including a table of contents, as well as a list of numbered tables and figures
- ❑ Rapid browse and search facilities
- ❑ Zoom facility for magnifying graphics or for increasing page size for easy readability
- ❑ Cut and paste capabilities
- ❑ Printing facility
- ❑ Reduced volume for easy filing/portability

Working environment: DOS, Windows or Macintosh.

Subscription:	FF 1 800	US$317	£200	DM 545
Single issue:	FF 130	US$24	£14	DM 40

Complete 1994/1995 series on CD-ROM:

	FF 2 000	US$365	£220	DM 600

Please send your order to OECD Electronic Editions or, preferably, to the Centre or bookshop with whom you placed your initial order for this Economic Survey.

OECD
ECONOMIC
SURVEYS

1994-1995

TURKEY

ORGANISATION FOR ECONOMIC CO-OPERATION AND DEVELOPMENT

ORGANISATION FOR ECONOMIC CO-OPERATION AND DEVELOPMENT

Pursuant to Article 1 of the Convention signed in Paris on 14th December 1960, and which came into force on 30th September 1961, the Organisation for Economic Co-operation and Development (OECD) shall promote policies designed:

- to achieve the highest sustainable economic growth and employment and a rising standard of living in Member countries, while maintaining financial stability, and thus to contribute to the development of the world economy;
- to contribute to sound economic expansion in Member as well as non-member countries in the process of economic development; and
- to contribute to the expansion of world trade on a multilateral, non-discriminatory basis in accordance with international obligations.

The original Member countries of the OECD are Austria, Belgium, Canada, Denmark, France, Germany, Greece, Iceland, Ireland, Italy, Luxembourg, the Netherlands, Norway, Portugal, Spain, Sweden, Switzerland, Turkey, the United Kingdom and the United States. The following countries became Members subsequently through accession at the dates indicated hereafter: Japan (28th April 1964), Finland (28th January 1969), Australia (7th June 1971), New Zealand (29th May 1973) and Mexico (18th May 1994). The Commission of the European Communities takes part in the work of the OECD (Article 13 of the OECD Convention).

Publié également en français.

Table of contents

Tables

Diagrams

Annexes

BASIC STATISTICS OF TURKEY

THE LAND

Area (thousand sq. km)	779	Major cities, 1990	
Agricultural area (thousand sq. km)	275	(thousand inhabitants):	
Forests (thousand sq. km)	202	Istanbul	7 309
		Ankara	3 237
		Izmir	2 695

THE PEOPLE

Population, 1993 (million)	59.5	Civilian labour force, 1993 (thousands)	20 232
Per sq. km, 1993	76	Civilian employment	18 702
Annual average rate of change		Agriculture, forestry, fishing	8 397
of population, 1993	1.9	Industry	2 825
		Construction	1 140
		Services	6 340

PRODUCTION

GDP, 1993 (TL billion)	1 913 150	Origin of GDP, 1993 (per cent):	
Per head (US$)	2 932	Agriculture, forestry, fishing	14.4
Gross fixed investment, 1993 (TL billion)	484 588	Industry	25.4
Per cent of GDP	25.0	Construction	7.1
Per head (US$)	743	Services	53.1

THE GOVERNMENT

Public consumption, 1993 (per cent of GDP)	13.3	Public debt, end-1993 (per cent of GDP)	36.8
Central government current revenue,		Domestic	19.3
1993 (per cent of GDP)	18.4	Foreign	17.5

FOREIGN TRADE

Commodity exports, 1993, fob		Commodity imports, 1993, cif	
(per cent of GDP)	8.8	(per cent of GDP)	16.9
Main exports (per cent of total exports):		Main imports (per cent of total imports):	
Agriculture	15.5	Investment goods	32.5
Mining	1.6	of which: machinery	29.0
Industry	82.9	Consumption goods	14.0
		Raw materials	53.5

THE CURRENCY

Monetary unit: Turkish lira		Currency unit per US$,	
		average of daily figures:	
		1992	6 861
		1993	10 966
		1994	29 778

Note: An international comparison of certain basic statistics is given in an annex table.

This Survey is based on the Secretariat's study prepared for the annual review of Turkey by the Economic and Development Review Committee on 7th February 1995.

•

After revisions in the light of discussions during the review, final approval of the Survey for publication was given by the Committee on 24 February 1995.

•

The previous Survey of Turkey was issued in March 1994.

Introduction

Shortly after the Committee's previous review of Turkey, early 1994 saw a run on the Turkish lira, triggered by a loss of confidence in economic policy and concerns over the country's ability to service its external debt. The 1994 financial crisis was the culmination of years of growing macroeconomic imbalances and failure to correct the root causes of high fiscal deficits. In 1993, domestic demand grew by over 11 per cent, and the related overheating was reflected in a sharp widening in the current-account deficit and inflation accelerating to 60 per cent. Rather than declining as had been envisaged in budget plans, the public-sector borrowing requirement (PSBR) instead increased further to over 12 per cent of GDP in 1993. The recourse to Central Bank financing of the PSBR led to a loss of control over the money supply, and the effects of this were exacerbated by wide-scale currency substitution, which reduced the demand for lira-denominated money, ultimately provoking a sharp depreciation.

On 5 April 1994, an ambitious stabilisation programme was launched to halve the ratio of the PSBR to GDP in 1994 and to accelerate structural reform. A reduction of some 4 to 5 percentage points in the PSBR/GDP ratio may have been achieved, and a further reduction is targeted in the 1995 budget. Output has dropped sharply since April. But the current account has swung into surplus, external debt service obligations have been fully respected, foreign exchange reserves rebuilt, and there are signs that the drop in economic activity has stopped. Following a brief calm, strong inflationary pressures re-emerged from September raising year-on-year wholesale price inflation to over 150 per cent by January 1995. Chapter I reviews recent economic developments and presents the economic outlook for the coming two years.

Chapter II discusses salient features of the policies leading up to the early 1994 currency crisis, and the measures taken to restore financial market stability. It then examines the challenge of establishing fiscal sustainability and lowering inflation in both the short and medium term. In the short run, the switch from money to debt financing of the PSBR could see steeply rising debt-to-GDP ratios, the more so if high risk premia on Turkish-lira-denominated debt are not reduced. Risk premia are likely to fall only as confidence is built up through a track record of achieving fiscal and inflation targets.

Medium-term fiscal stabilisation will require vigorous structural reform of large loss-making State economic enterprises, and the tax and social security systems. Progress in these and other areas of reform is sketched out in Chapter III. Notwithstanding delays in privatisation, signs of change are emerging, as the financial crisis and imminent customs union with the EU oblige the government to address the constraints of a bloated and inefficient public sector. The need to raise Turkey's comparatively low basic health and education standards is another compelling reason to rationalise public-sector operations and to re-examine government spending priorities. Conclusions of the Survey are presented in Chapter IV.

I. Recent economic developments and prospects

Overview

The Turkish economy registered high rates of growth from 1980 to 1993, aided by the outward-looking reorientation of trade policy in 1980 and structural reform. But macroeconomic imbalances became pronounced after 1988, as monetary financing of chronic fiscal deficits engendered inflation of more than 50 per cent a year and a weakening external position, culminating in an exchange market crisis in early 1994. An ambitious stabilisation package was launched on 5 April 1994. By December, noteworthy progress had been made in cutting the PSBR and shifting the current account into surplus. Foreign debt payments were fully met and financial market stability restored. But real GDP fell by over 11 per cent in the year to the second quarter of 1994, although the decline moderated in the subsequent quarter. Labour market conditions have deteriorated and inflation remains a major concern. Following a summer calm, inflation picked up briskly in the autumn to above programme targets. This chapter surveys salient features of the economic developments up to the 1994 exchange market crisis, progress made since the April programme, and prospects in the coming two years.

The boom and bust

Demand and output

GDP growth was buoyant in 1992 and 1993,[1] reflecting large public and private-sector real wage increases and lax macroeconomic policies. By end-1993, the economy was overheating (Diagram 1, top left panel). Domestic demand soared by 11¾ per cent in 1993, import volumes jumped by 36 per cent and GDP grew by 7.5 per cent (compared with a growth of potential output of close to 5 per cent). In the first quarter of 1994, GDP expanded by a still robust 4.3 per cent (year-on-year). But drops in real wages (in the wake of depreciation and

3

Diagram 1. **KEY ASPECTS OF ECONOMIC ACTIVITY**

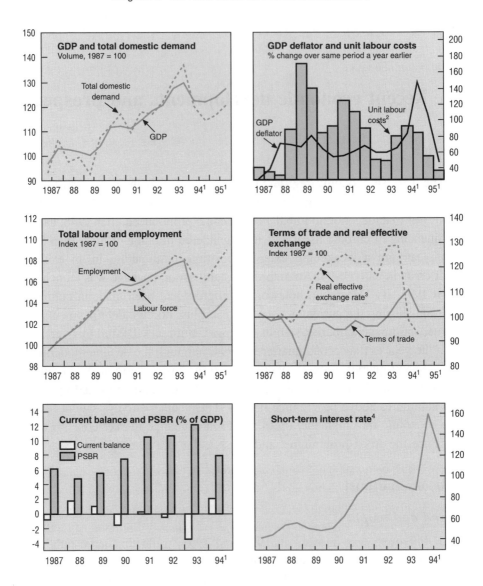

1. Estimates for 1994 and OECD projections for 1995.
2. Total economy.
3. Calculated using consumer price inflation relative to Turkeys's trading partners.
4. Three-month treasury bill.
Source: OECD, *National Accounts, Main Economic Indicators,* and estimates.

public-sector price hikes) led to a sharp retrenchment. In the second quarter of 1994, consumer spending and investment dropped by 10 and 22 per cent, respectively, and domestic demand plummeted by 19 per cent; there was a massive swing in net exports, with a 33 per cent drop in imports and a 8 per cent rise in exports, leaving GDP 11.3 per cent down on a year earlier. The drop in domestic demand moderated in the third quarter, with a continuing swing to net exports – but GDP was still down by almost 8 per cent on its year earlier level.

Agricultural output fell 2.2 per cent in 1993, but still represented 15 per cent of GDP; it fell further in the first two quarters of 1994 due to poor harvests and acreage restrictions on some crops (see Chapter III). By contrast, industrial output increased by 8.2 per cent in 1993, raising its share in GDP to 27 per cent. Industrial output expanded further in the first quarter of 1994, but dropped by almost 12 per cent in the second quarter (Table 1 and Diagram 2). This reflected a

Table 1. **Supply and use of resources**

	1993 Share of GDP in current prices	1991	1992	1993	1994 Estimate [1]	1995 Programme [1]
		Percentage volume changes				
Supply						
Agriculture	15.8	–0.2	3.9	0.5	–2.5	2.5
Industry	23.8	3.3	6.8	10.4	–1.9	4.9
Construction	7.5	0.9	5.9	7.9		
Services	52.9	0.5	7.0	4.0	–3.2 [3]	4.3 [3]
GDP	100.0	0.9	6.0	7.5	–2.8	4.2
Demand						
Private consumption	67.4	1.9	3.3	7.1	–3.2	2.2
Public consumption	13.3	4.5	3.8	4.8	–2.8	3.1
Investment	25.3	1.2	4.3	21.7	–15.7	6.1
Final domestic demand	106.0	1.9	3.6	10.6		
Stockbuilding [2]	1.1	–2.9	1.6	1.2	–3.1	1.9
Total domestic demand	107.2	–0.9	5.2	11.7		
Exports of goods and services	14.2	3.7	11.0	7.7		
Imports of goods and services	20.0	–5.2	10.9	35.8		
Foreign balance [2]	–5.9	1.8	–0.3	–6.2	5.7	–0.7
Statistical discrepancy [2]	–1.3	0.1	1.0	1.7		
GDP	100.0	0.9	6.0	7.5	–2.8	4.2

1. Data from State Planning Organisation.
2. Contribution to growth.
3. Including construction.
Source: State Institute of Statistics, *Turkish Economy, Statistics and Analysis*, and State Planning Organisation.

Diagram 2. **INDUSTRIAL PRODUCTION**

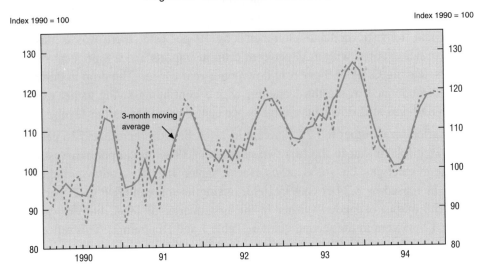

Source: State Institute of Statistics, *Monthly Bulletin*.

particularly sharp drop in public and private investment (Table 2), but also the liquidation of excess stocks. Once the latter was finished, industrial production and capacity utilisation recovered in the third quarter,[2] supported by strong export demand, following the large real depreciation. Services (construction, tourism, transportation and communications, finance, commerce and social services) make up the bulk of GDP. Output growth in 1993 was rapid in tourism, transportation and construction, but fell in these sectors in the second and third quarters of 1994.

An important difficulty in analysing the real economy is that timely data are largely confined to the formal economy, which excludes a significant element of economic activity.[3] Output, income and expenditure data are consistent with strong output growth in 1993, a sharp drop in the second quarter of 1994 and a modest recovery in activity in the third quarter. But inflation remains surprisingly brisk in view of the measured drop in output and demand – and growth of real M2Y[4] remains quite sustained, suggesting that output and demand (notably of the

Table 2. **Gross fixed investment by sector**

Volume, 1993 prices

	1993 Share	1991	1992	1993	1994 Estimate	1995 Programme
				Percentage changes		
Private sector						
Agriculture	3.2	−10.2	0.8	38.1	−18.1	5.4
Mining	0.9	0.5	−9.5	15.5	22.9	5.4
Manufacturing	23.6	−1.4	0.2	25.6	−16.5	3.9
Energy	0.5	46.0	−47.1	−2.0	−15.1	236.0
Transportation	18.8	3.0	41.2	69.7	−42.5	16.5
Tourism	2.4	−5.0	−20.9	−17.5	−5.2	−5.8
Housing	44.9	−0.2	0.1	20.0	4.5	3.4
Education	0.8	15.9	6.6	18.6	−2.6	17.3
Health	1.3	45.5	7.1	17.0	−2.8	8.1
Other	3.7	0.6	5.8	9.0	−3.1	4.1
Total	100.0 (71.5)	0.2	3.1	26.8	−10.6	6.2
Public sector						
Agriculture	10.0	12.9	−13.6	9.5	−20.5	7.4
Mining	2.6	3.8	4.1	−21.3	−34.4	11.4
Manufacturing	3.3	17.7	12.7	−33.5	−39.7	40.9
Energy	12.5	−18.7	−9.1	−8.8	−8.1	22.9
Transportation	39.0	9.3	6.3	9.3	−35.9	−13.1
Tourism	1.9	33.3	12.6	25.7	−37.4	17.2
Housing	2.4	−47.7	29.9	−2.6	8.6	−35.5
Education	9.8	−4.6	27.8	37.0	−32.7	8.5
Health	4.0	−8.0	35.9	30.6	−36.8	12.0
Other	14.6	7.8	20.5	6.0	−27.1	29.5
Total	100.0 (28.5)	1.4	6.1	5.6	−28.4	5.9
Total gross fixed investment	(100.0)	0.6	4.0	20.0	−15.7	6.1

Note: These data may not be fully compatible with national accounts data due to diffferences in classifications and in base period price deflators.
Source: State Planning Organisation.

informal economy) may be holding up better than indicated by official GDP data (Diagram 3).

Labour market

The dominant feature of the labour market in Turkey is rapid growth of the working-age population and the large proportion of lower age groups – implying

Diagram 3. **MONEY SUPPLY**

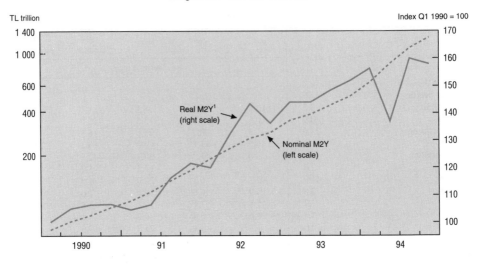

1. M2Y deflated by the wholesale price index. M2Y equals M2 plus domestic foreign exchange deposits.
Source: Central Bank of Turkey, *Monthly Statistical Bulletin,* and State Institute of Statistics, *Monthly Bulletin.*

that strong job creation is needed merely to hold the unemployment rate steady (see Chapter III). In 1993, the civilian labour force was 20.2 million, about 54.2 per cent of the population being over 15 years of age (Table 3). Total civilian employment in 1993 was 18.7 million, of which 44.9 per cent were employed in agriculture, 15.6 per cent in industry and 39.5 per cent in services. Household labour-force survey data for 1994 are not yet available.

Following the April measures, a number of redundancies and short-time work were announced. Around 45 000 net job losses were reported by the Ministry of Labour between January and June. The bulk of the labour market adjustment has so far been made in the private sector. The unemployment rate dropped from 7.9 per cent in 1992 to 7.6 per cent in 1993, but when underemployment is included, the figures reached about 15 and 14 per cent, respectively, in 1992 and 1993. Data for 1994 are not yet available, but official estimates indicate an unemployment rate of some 10.5 per cent coming on top of a further rise in underemployment to around 9.3 per cent.

Table 3. **Labour market indicators** [1]

	1970	1980	1990	1991	1992	1993	1970/89	1991	1992	1993
	Thousand						Percentage change over previous period			
Participation ratio (per cent)	68	63	57	56	56	54				
Civilian labour force	13 905	17 078	19 954	19 967	20 196	20 232	1.8	0.1	1.1	0.2
Civilian employment	13 034	15 702	18 364	18 420	18 600	18 702	1.7	0.3	1.0	0.5
As a percentage share										
Agriculture	63.2	53.2	47.5	47.3	44.0	44.9	0.2	-0.2	-6.3	2.8
Mining	1.2	1.2	1.1	1.0	0.9	0.7	1.0	-12.9	-9.3	-24.0
Manufacturing	10.3	13.1	13.9	14.4	15.2	14.4	3.5	3.6	7.2	-5.3
Construction	5.1	5.7	5.3	5.5	5.6	6.1	2.3	4.0	3.7	10.3
Trade	6.8	9.1	11.4	11.6	12.6	12.5	4.5	2.2	9.3	-0.5
Transport	3.2	3.9	4.4	4.2	4.5	4.8	3.6	-3.7	8.3	7.6
Other	10.2	13.7	16.4	16.0	17.2	16.6	4.0	-1.6	8.0	-3.0
Unemployment	871	1 376	1 590	1 547	1 596	1 530				
Unemployment rate	6.3	8.1	8.0	7.7	7.9	7.6				

1. For population aged 15 and over.
Source: State Institute of Statistics.

Costs and prices

A proximate cause of the foreign exchange crisis was the rise in consumer and wholesale price inflation from around 55 to some 65 per cent in the course of 1993 (Diagram 4). But the underlying reason was monetisation of the PSBR. The immediate effect of the stabilisation package was a further sharp increase in the price level, coming on top of a large nominal depreciation. The wholesale price index (WPI) increased by 32.8 per cent in April, raising the twelve-month increase from 74 per cent in March to 125 per cent (Table 4). Higher import prices may have accounted for about a quarter of the WPI rise in April, and the more than 50 per cent rise in administered SEEs prices for about one-half.[5] Excluding these factors, "underlying WPI inflation" may have been some 4 per cent a month.

July and August saw a sharp easing in inflation pressures. WPI inflation came down to less than 2 per cent a month, raising optimism that the large output gap and big cuts in the PSBR could hold inflation in line with the forecast of less than 3 per cent a month in the second half of 1994.[6] In the event, September through December saw a resurgence of inflation, with the monthly rise in the WPI and CPI averaging 6.7 and 7.8 per cent, respectively. Broadly-basedpressure

Diagram 4. **INFLATION DEVELOPMENTS**

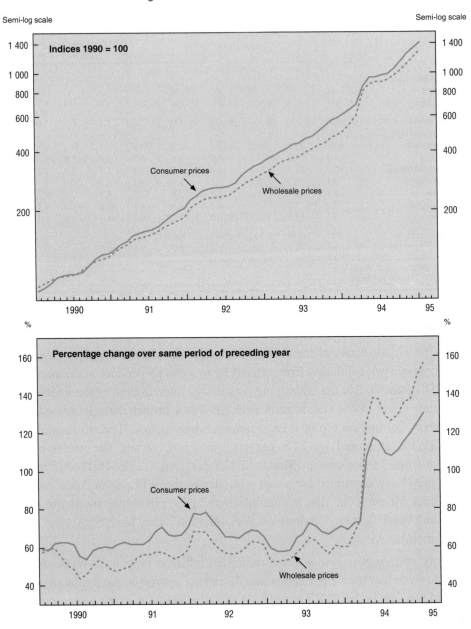

Source: OECD, *Main Economic Indicators.*

10

Table 4. **Prices**[1]

Percentage change over previous year, annual and quarterly averages
(Base year 1987 = 100)

	General index			Wholesale prices				Consumer prices	
	Total	Public	Private	Agriculture	Mining	Manufacturing	Energy	General	Food
Weights	(100.0)	(27.74)	(72.26)	(23.03)	(2.54)	(69.80)	(4.62)	(100.0)	(32.1)
1988	70.5	70.3	70.5	44.1	64.1	81.5	40.9	73.7	83.2
1989	64.0	64.2	63.9	71.7	65.0	61.6	69.2	63.2	69.3
1990	52.3	56.7	50.6	70.6	48.7	46.9	56.5	60.3	64.3
1991	55.3	61.3	53.0	50.8	63.2	55.3	75.1	66.0	67.1
1992	62.1	65.2	60.8	62.7	61.6	59.7	97.7	70.1	71.3
1993	58.4	54.5	60.1	62.2	56.7	56.6	67.8	66.1	63.5
1994	120.7	122.5	119.8	97.8	132.8	129.4	102.3	106.3	110.0
Q1	67.8	63.0	69.7	70.6	67.3	66.8	69.2	72.1	72.5
Q2	133.9	149.0	127.7	94.1	146.6	148.0	119.7	113.8	120.2
Q3	128.3	132.2	126.5	91.4	157.8	140.2	117.0	109.5	107.4
Q4	141.3	135.0	144.0	126.3	145.7	149.8	99.4	120.6	129.9
October	136.9	127.7	140.9	123.2	151.7	143.7	104.8	116.3	124.9
November	137.0	127.5	141.0	121.2	141.5	146.1	92.8	119.7	127.8
December	149.6	149.4	149.6	134.0	144.2	159.1	100.9	125.5	136.2
1995									
January	156.8	151.9	158.9	146.4	146.9	167.7	81.1	130.7	144.0

1. In January 1990, the State Institute of Statistics introduced new weights for both wholesale and consumer price indices, and changed the base year of the consumer price index from 1978-79 to 1987. In January 1991, the base year for the wholesale index was changed from 1981 to 1987.
Source: State Institute of Statistics, *Wholesale and Consumer Price Indices Monthly Bulletin.*

11

was evident in the monthly rise in the private-sector WPI of some 7½ per cent.[7] Agricultural prices rose by 11.7 per cent owing to a poor harvest, while private-sector manufacturing prices rose by 5.8 per cent, partly in response to higher export prices and a drop in the exchange rate towards end-August. Inflation remained pronounced in early 1995 with monthly rises in the WPI and CPI of 8.4 and 6.8 per cent respectively in January.

Wage data cover only a small fraction of the labour force, but imply that real wages for dependent employees fell by some 15 to 20 per cent in 1994.[8] Income for the self-employed are difficult to assess. Agricultural income probably fell only modestly, in view of higher agricultural prices following the large depreciation. By contrast, non-wage income may have fallen significantly, albeit from a very buoyant 1993 outturn. There was a big shift to interest income, in view of unusually high prevailing real rates of interest.

The principal difficulty in lowering inflation is to overcome inertia by achieving a decisive break in inflation expectations. As in other countries, expectations are dominated by past performance. Current interest rates on 3-month Treasury bills (of over 100 cent per annum) indicate a major dichotomy between private-sector expectations and the government's forecast of lowering inflation to 22.5 per cent by the end of 1995. Private-sector expectations are adaptive, and probably adjust slowly. Inflation has been above 50 per cent since 1987 and the April programme raised WPI inflation in the short run to close to 125 per cent. Notwithstanding high overall real-wage flexibility, slowly adapting expectations imply that the output costs of achieving low inflation could be severe. (In the event, in January 1995 the government's end year 1995 inflation forecast was raised to just under 40 per cent, in view of stronger underlying inflation.)

A key issue is whether the latest resurgence in inflation was an aberration or a reflection of more fundamental factors. To some extent, the recent rebound reflected temporary factors (e.g. agricultural shortages due to a poor harvest). But, although the 1994 budget targets were broadly met and monetary financing of the PSBR and real wages were significantly reduced, monetary policy was insufficiently tight between July and October. Over this period, foreign reserves recovered sharply, excess liquidity was not sufficiently sterilised, and the nominal exchange rate dropped sharply in late August. The late summer recovery in industrial production also allowed producers to raise prices, in the absence of keen foreign competition.

The OECD Secretariat's analysis indicates that the rebound in WPI inflation in September-December can be well explained in terms of the contemporaneous effects of currency depreciation (from late August through mid-October as interest rates fell) and the quick (5-month) pass-through of broad money (M2) to inflation (see Annex I for a technical description). This empirical relation suggests the apparently dominant role of monetary variables in determining inflation even in the short run. But other effects, such as cost pressure and capacity utilisation may be masked when money supply is growing rapidly.

External developments

A surge in imports led to a widening of the current account deficit from 0.6 per cent of GDP in 1992 to 3.9 per cent of GDP in 1993. A major success of the April 1994 programme has been the rapid restoration of external balance. A large part of the improvement in the current account reflected the sharp drop in domestic demand. But a substantial drop in the real effective exchange rate (of 30 per cent in the twelve months to October) (Diagram 5) must also have contributed to the swing.

Diagram 5. **REAL EFFECTIVE EXCHANGE RATE**[1]

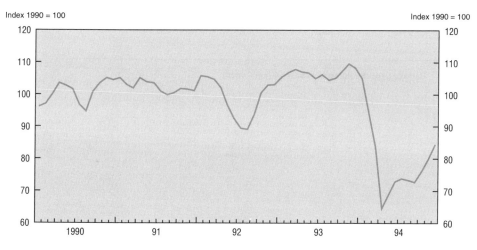

Index 1990 = 100

Index 1990 = 100

1. Calculated using consumer price inflation relative to Turkey's trading partners.
Source: OECD.

13

Diagram 6. **FOREIGN TRADE DEVELOPMENTS**

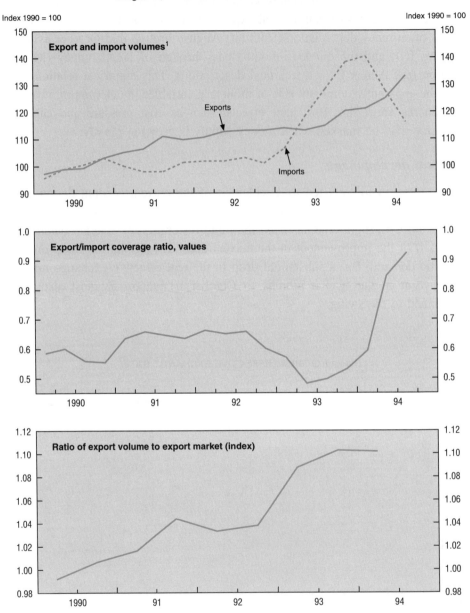

1. Using four-quarter moving average on quantity indices.
Source: State Institute of Statistics, *Summary of Monthly Trade,* and OECD.

The swing in the current account, despite adverse short-run ''J'' curve effects, was surprisingly rapid. Although there was a drop in the terms of trade (Diagram 1), this was modest, as Turkish exporters are price takers, and export and import contracts are largely denominated in foreign currencies. In addition to the sharp contraction in imports, export performance has been dynamic, underlining the quick response of the private sector to improved profitability. By the third quarter, exports were 35 per cent higher than a year before, and imports down by 27 per cent. The export/import coverage ratio rose from 0.65 in the first quarter to around 0.9 in the third quarter (Diagram 6, panel 2). Further export market gains and lower import penetration are expected, as supplier-customer relations continue to adjust to the lower level of the real exchange rate. All in all, the current account registered a surplus of US$2.2 billion from January to September 1994, compared with a deficit of US$4.8 billion in the same period a year earlier (Table 5 and Diagram 7).

Table 5. **Balance of payments**

$ million

	1991	1992	1993	1994 Estimate [1]	1995 Programme [1]
Current account					
Export (fob)	13 667	14 891	15 610	17 800	19 850
Imports (fob)	21 007	23 081	29 772	22 440	26 370
Trade balance	-7 340	-8 190	-14 162	-4 640	-6 520
Services, credit	9 315	10 451	11 843	11 450	12 300
of which: Tourism	2 654	3 639	3 959	4 000	4 500
Services, debit	6 816	7 262	7 829	8 150	8 900
Private transfers, net	2 854	3 147	3 035	2 800	3 000
of which: Workers' remittances	2 819	3 008	2 919	2 700	2 900
Official transfers, net	2 245	912	733	630	550
Current balance	258	-942	-6 380	2 090	430
Capital account					
Long-term capital	623	2 252	5 909	573	2 100
Direct investment	783	779	622	435	800
Portfolio investment	623	2 411	3 917	788	1 750
Other	-783	-938	1 370	-650	-450
Short-term capital	-3 020	1 396	3 054	-3 870	-1 430
Errors and omissions	940	-1 222	-2 275	1 567	0
Overall balance	-1 029 [2]	1 484	308	360	1 100

1. State Planning Organisation estimates.
2. Including $170 million for counterpart items.
Source: Central Bank of Turkey, *Quarterly Bulletin*, and State Planning Organisation.

Diagram 7. **CURRENT ACCOUNT AND EXTERNAL DEBT**
% of GDP

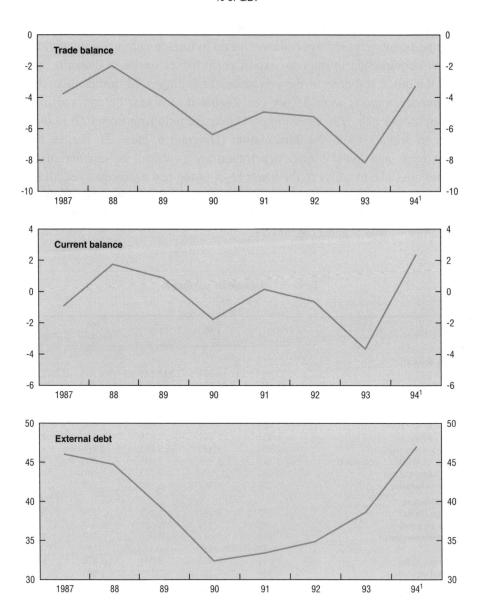

1. Estimates.
Source: Central Bank of Turkey and OECD.

16

In 1993, the current account deficit of US$6.4 billion and debt repayments of US$4.4 billion were largely financed by foreign borrowing.[9] For 1994, foreign debt service was some US$9.5 billion[10]. The downgrading of Turkey's sovereign credit-rating in January 1994 limited new foreign borrowing to US$721 million (two Samurai bond issues in February). The immediate mechanical effect of the depreciation of the TL was to raise the foreign debt burden.[11] Debt service as a percent of exports of goods and services plus private and official unrequited transfers rose from 25 to 28 per cent (Table 6).

The increase in the debt service ratio raised concerns about Turkey's ability to meet its external commitments without debt rescheduling. In the event, the

Table 6. **External debt of Turkey**

Disbursed debt – end of period

$ million

	1989	1990	1991	1992	1993	1994 September[1]
Medium- and long-term debt	36 006	39 535	41 372	42 932	48 823	52 625
Multilateral creditors	8 740	9 564	10 069	9 160	8 674	9 022
Bilateral creditors	11 431	12 984	14 587	15 035	18 153	19 100
Commercial banks	10 269	10 720	10 992	12 956	15 706	16 561
Private lenders	5 566	6 267	5 724	5 781	6 290	7 942
Short-term debt	5 745	9 500	9 117	12 660	18 533	12 154
Credits	2 950	5 524	6 134	10 065	15 436	8 840
Deposits	2 795	3 976	2 983	2 595	3 097	3 314
Total debt	41 751	49 035	50 489	55 592	67 356	64 779
Memorandum items (per cent)						
Total debt/GDP	39.0	32.5	33.4	35.0	38.7	–
Medium- and long-term debt/GDP	33.6	26.2	27.4	27.0	28.0	–
Short-term debt/GDP	5.4	6.3	6.0	8.0	10.6	–
Short-term/total debt	13.8	19.4	18.1	22.8	27.5	18.8
Total debt/foreign exchange revenue	185.8	185.2	179.6	189.1	215.7	–
Medium- and long-term debt by borrower as per cent of total debt						
General government	55.2	52.3	54.3	51.2	45.7	47.3
SEE's	10.5	9.8	10.3	9.2	8.1	8.1
Central bank	16.7	14.9	12.9	11.1	9.8	12.7
Private sector	3.8	3.7	4.5	5.7	8.9	8.2
Debt service/GDP	6.5	4.8	5.0	5.1	4.5	–
Debt service/foreign exchange revenue	30.8	27.2	26.8	27.5	25.2	28.6
Average maturity (year)	15.0	15.1	14.6	14.0	12.5	12.8
Average spread over LIBOR	1.2	0.9	1.0	1.6	..	..

1. Provisional.
Source: Central Bank of Turkey, *Quarterly Bulletin.*

rapid shift in the current account, and a reversal in short-term capital flows, not only allowed debt service to be fully met, but also allowed a rapid rebuilding of foreign reserves to pre-crisis levels. Turkey was taken off credit watch by the major international rating agencies in late summer after the signing of stand-by credit arrangements with the IMF. In November, a US$350 million loan was obtained, secured on US exports to Turkey (backed by the US Ex-Im Bank). The favourable rates obtained by this loan indicate that a modest re-entry into foreign capital markets is feasible in 1995.

Short-term economic prospects

The economic outlook over the coming two years sketched out below is based on the following technical assumptions:

- Monetary conditions will remain sufficiently tight in the coming two years to rein in growth of the money supply broadly to attain the revised 1995 official inflation forecast and yet lower inflation in 1996.
- The government's non-interest spending limits announced in the 1995 draft budget will be strictly adhered to and its revenue targets will be reached.
- The real exchange rate remains unchanged from its level prevailing on 2 November 1994.
- Oil prices average US$15.60 a barrel in the second half of 1994 and remain unchanged in real terms thereafter.
- Growth of Turkish export markets is in the 7 to 8 per cent range in the coming two years.

A modest export-led recovery is projected in 1995. Export volumes, which led recovery in the second half of 1994, are expected to grow by 15 per cent in 1995 (Table 7), implying further gains in market share. Real wages declined significantly in 1994 and, together with high real interest rates, are likely to make for continuing subdued domestic demand. Consumer spending is projected to grow by 1 1/2 per cent and investment to fall by 1 per cent.

The OECD Secretariat's GDP projections for 1995 of 2.8 per cent are somewhat lower than the revised 3.8 per cent estimate prepared by the State Planning Organisation (SPO). The SPO projects a more rapid recovery in domes-

Table 7. **Projections for 1995 and 1996**

Percentage changes, volume (1987 prices)

	1991		1994 Estimate	1995	1996
	Current prices TL trillion	Per cent of GDP		Projections	
Private consumption	434.4	68.9	−4.7	2.0	3.5
Public consumption	78.3	12.4	−1.2	−1.5	1.7
Gross fixed investment	149.3	23.7	−23.7	−2.5	4.3
Final domestic demand	661.7	105.0	−9.8	0.7	3.6
Stockbuilding [1]	−6.2	−1.0	−2.8	0.5	0.5
Total domestic demand	655.5	104.0	−12.3	1.2	4.1
Exports of goods and services	87.2	13.8	15.0	15.0	13.0
Imports of goods and services	104.8	16.6	−20.0	7.5	11.0
GDP at market prices	630.1	100.0	−4.8	2.8	4.6
GDP implicit price deflator			120.0	70.0	40.0
Memorandum items					
Consumer prices			110.0	70.0	20.0
Unemployment rate			10.9	12.0	12.5
Current balance ($ billion)			3.0	4.0	4.5
Current balance (% of GDP)			2.4	2.8	2.6

1. Change as a percentage of GDP in previous period.
Source: OECD.

tic demand, with fixed investment rising by 6 per cent, and public and private consumption by 3 and 2 per cent, respectively. Both projections are for 12-monthly inflation of just below 40 per cent by the end of 1995.

For 1996, the OECD projects that the recovery will become more broadly based, with the real depreciation and customs union with the European Union stimulating investment in sectors exposed to foreign competition.[12] GDP growth is projected to pick up to 4.8 per cent, still leaving considerable slack on the labour market. Inflation is projected to continue on a declining path and the current account to remain in surplus in both 1995 and 1996.

The risks attached to these projections are large. A major uncertainty is the degree of success the authorities will have in implementing the 1995 budget programme, and how quickly private-sector expectations adapt to official inflation forecasts. The projected decline in inflation will require monthly inflation averaging just under 3 per cent in the course of 1995, roughly half the rate expected by some private sector agents. This credibility gap is projected to be reduced on the assumption that tight macroeconomic policies are maintained and a consistent track record of meeting PSBR and official inflation forecasts is established. Stepped-up structural reform to support medium-term consolidation is also assumed, following an extended period of limited progress.

II. Re-establishing macroeconomic balance

The April 1994 stabilisation programme and the 1995 budget are essential first steps in the realignment of economic policy and restoration of macroeconomic balance. Establishing the preconditions for sustained medium-term economic growth will require on-going, vigorous action on both macroeconomic and microeconomic policy fronts. This chapter discusses the task facing macroeconomic policy over the medium term to establish low inflation, fiscal sustainability and better growth prospects.

Macroeconomic policies up to the Spring 1994 crisis

The early 1994 crisis occurred against a background of progressive increases in the PSBR from some $3\frac{1}{2}$ per cent of GDP in 1986 to over 12 per cent in 1993 despite numerous deficit reduction plans and buoyant economic activity. Since the late 1980s, fiscal policy has often been procyclical up until the crisis of Spring 1994. In 1991, when the output gap was close to zero, the PSBR was over 10 per cent of GDP. The cyclically-adjusted PSBR increased further in 1992 and 1993. Fiscal policy was particularly lax in 1993. Although the PSBR was targeted at $6\frac{1}{2}$ per cent of GDP, it rose to over 12 per cent of GDP,[13] at a time when GDP was estimated by the Secretariat to be some 4 per cent above potential output (see Annex IV). Further, high rates of inflation led to increasing foreign currency substitution for the Turkish lira. This restricted seigniorage gains (Diagram 8) and necessitated growing recourse to Central Bank financing of the PSBR (rising from 0.5 per cent of GDP in 1986 to 2.6 per cent in 1993).

From 1990 to 1992, the overriding goal of the Central Bank was to restore control of its own balance sheet. To achieve this goal a monetary programme was announced, targeting key balance-sheet components such as Central Bank money, total domestic assets, and total domestic liabilities. Combined with lax

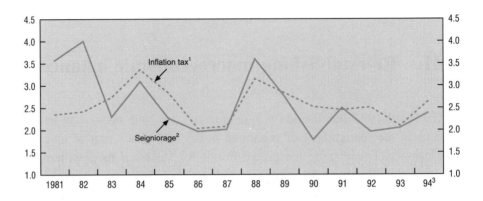

Diagram 8. **SEIGNIORAGE AND INFLATION TAX**
As per cent of GDP

1. Consumer price inflation multiplied by the ratio reserve money of previous period over GDP.
2. Change in reserve money divided by GDP.
3. Estimates.
Source: Central Bank of Turkey and OECD.

fiscal policy, this resulted in high real interest rates and an appreciating real exchange rate, with consequences for interest costs of the public debt and for external competitiveness. With no support from fiscal policy, the authorities did not announce a monetary programme for 1993 and instead focused their attention on maintaining orderly exchange-market conditions. The inability of the Central Bank to control its balance sheet and hence high-powered base money[14] quickly led to large increases in broad money: in 1993, M2 grew by 50 per cent and M2Y (which includes domestic deposits of foreign currency) by 78 per cent – the difference in growth rates reflecting the classic "run" to foreign currencies as a hedge against inflation. The share of Turkish lira deposits in M2Y declined from 80 per cent in early 1991 to 53 per cent at the end of 1993 (Diagram 9).

In late 1993, the draft 1994 budget was presented to Parliament. Despite growing macroeconomic imbalances, the PSBR was programmed to be over 10 per cent of GDP (albeit aiming at reducing the primary deficit by 2.5 per cent of GDP), with Central Bank financing of the deficit exceeding 2 per cent of GDP. In January 1994, Turkey's sovereign debt rating was lowered to below invest-

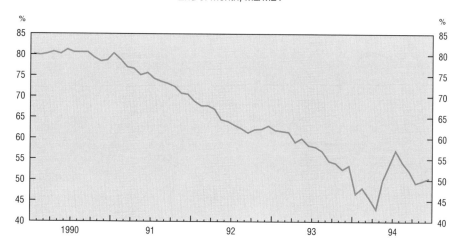

Diagram 9. **CURRENCY SUBSTITUTION**
End of month, M2/M2Y[1]

1.   M2Y equals M2 plus domestic foreign exchange deposits.
Source: Central Bank of Turkey, *Monthly Statistical Bulletin.*

ment grade paper by two leading rating agencies, triggering a run on the Turkish lira and a further shift into foreign currencies. Financial market confidence weakened sharply as Treasury bill auctions were cancelled to avoid paying higher interest rates. By the end of March, the Treasury had drawn all its quota of Central Bank advances for 1994, and was effectively cut off from borrowing on domestic or foreign capital markets. From December 1993 to April 1994, the share of domestic currency deposits in M2Y fell from 53 per cent to 42 per cent.

Against a background of deteriorating confidence, the lira plummeted (Diagram 10). The average monthly increase in the price of foreign currency accelerated from 4.2 per cent between June and December 1993 to 8 per cent in January and 62 per cent in April 1994 – when the 12-month increase reached 232 per cent.[15] A number of commercial banks holding short positions in foreign currency were wrong-footed by the run on the lira, and faced large capital losses.[16] With the economy facing the spectre of spiralling inflation and financial market instability, a stabilisation package was announced on 5 April, one week after the local elections.

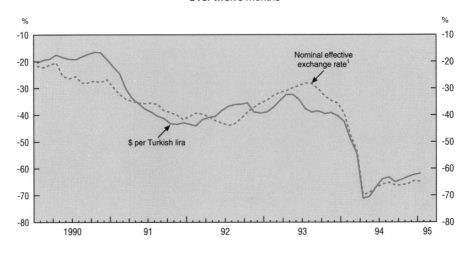

Diagram 10. **DEPRECIATION OF THE TURKISH LIRA**

Over twelve months

1. Trade-weighted index.
Source: OECD.

The authorities' immediate priority was to restore financial market stability. Following the placing of three small banks under receivership,[17] the authorities took the radical step of extending guarantees to 100 per cent of individuals' bank deposits. The Central Bank also extended its control over the financial system by extending reserve and liquidity requirements to asset-backed securities, as well as deposits and non-deposit liabilities excluding capital and other items. These regulations were extended to investment banks and special finance institutions. Other measures were taken to encourage the holding of TL. These included: applying lower reserve requirements on TL deposits than on foreign exchange deposits (8 per cent and 10 per cent, respectively); and introducing seven-day TL-notice accounts to compete with foreign exchange accounts.

In the event, the banking system weathered this shock. Only a few Turkish banks have yet to comply with BIS minimum capital adequacy ratios. In addition, the Banking Law incorporates the European Union's directives on lending limits and consolidated supervision. As regards financial market regulatory controls, the most controversial was the decision to provide 100 per cent insurance for bank deposits to individuals. Albeit justified in the context of an incipient run on the banks, such a guarantee can incur problems of "moral hazard",[18] and study is underway to improve these arrangements.

April 1994 programme

The April stabilisation programme is akin to those adopted by a number of countries in the past two decades.[19] Some programmes collapsed very quickly (*e.g.* Argentina and Brazil in the mid-1980s), while others were successful (Chile, Bolivia, Mexico, Israel). One lesson from these experiences is that successful stabilisation programmes require quick and firm control over public sector deficits, and in particular a halt to the use of money creation to finance public borrowing. The April programme thus put in place a large front-loaded fiscal correction, with the primary public sector balance swinging from a deficit of some 6.2 per cent of GDP in 1993 to near balance in 1994 (Table 8), though the total PSBR is still some 7.5 per cent of GDP.

Table 8. **Public sector borrowing requirement**

	1990	1991	1992	1993	1994 Programme
Budget balances (TL trillion)					
Public sector	−30.9	−67.5	−123.5	−240.9	−312.6
Consolidated budget	−12.0	−33.5	−47.4	−133.9	−192.0
Budget balances (% of GDP)					
Public sector	7.8	10.6	11.2	12.5	10.6
Consolidated budget	3.0	5.3	4.3	6.9	6.5
State economic enterprises	4.2	3.7	4.5	3.6	2.6
Local administrations	0.0	0.3	0.8	0.6	0.2
Social security institutions	−0.3	0.1	0.2	0.6	0.9
Extra-budgetary funds [1]	0.8	1.2	1.4	0.5	0.4
Financing of PSBR (% of GDP)					
Central Bank	0.1	1.7	1.6	2.1	1.8
Foreign borrowing, net	0.9	0.4	1.5	0.6	0.5
Domestic borrowing, net	6.5	8.3	7.6	9.5	8.2

1. Consolidated financial accounts of eleven extra-budgetary funds. SEEs in the process of privatisation which have been transferred to the Public Participation Administration are included in EBFs.
Source: State Planning Organisation, and OECD estimates.

Diagram 11. **OVERVIEW OF THE STABILISATION STRATEGY**

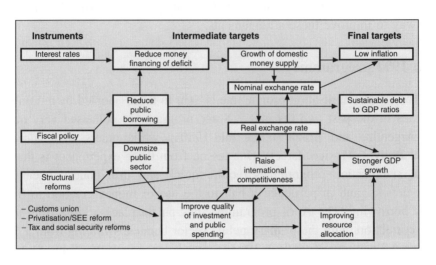

Source: OECD.

A schematic presentation of the stabilisation strategy is shown in Diagram 11. Final targets are indicated, along with policy instruments and intermediate targets to attain these, as well as feedback effects. Macroeconomic policy was oriented towards reducing domestic absorption and locking in a large real depreciation, while structural reform would boost potential output growth and fiscal consolidation in the medium term. This programme formed the basis for the negotiations of a 14-month US$742 million stand-by arrangement with the IMF concluded in July. As part of the arrangement, the authorities announced several key quarterly performance targets to increase policy transparency and to show their commitment to meeting the programme's targets (see Table 9).

The principal April 1994 measures included:
- Immediate price increases for products of State economic enterprises (SEEs) ranging from 70 to 100 per cent, to be followed by a six-month price freeze;
- a number of one-off tax measures to yield TL 64 trillion (1.6 per cent of GDP);[20]

26

Table 9. **April programme targets and outcomes**

	Period	Target	Outturn
Budget deficit (TL trillion)	April-Sept.	34.5	19.0
Inflation (%)	Sept.		
Consumer prices		47.7	53.9
Wholesale prices		53.1	61.1
Average rate of TL per $	Sept.	35 700[1]	33 895
Foreign exchange reserves of Central Bank (excluding gold) ($ million)	Sept.	3 244	6 729
Net domestic assets of Central Bank (TL trillion)	Sept.	295.0	278.1

1. Upper limit.
Source: Data provided by the Turkish authorities.

- maintenance of nominal spending levels on government wages and salaries as specified in the 1994 budget, despite higher inflation, implying a significant reduction in public-sector real wages;
- a reduction in transfers to SEEs of TL 16 trillion;
- cuts in public investment.

In sum, the consolidated budget deficit for 1994 was planned to be almost halved, from TL 198 trillion to TL 103 trillion (2.6 per cent of GDP), while the total PSBR was targeted at 6.2 per cent of GDP. Two-thirds of the adjustment was foreseen on spending.

Structural initiatives (discussed in some detail in Chapter III) included measures to downsize the public sector and to improve its efficiency, notably through streamlined privatisation legislation, imposition of hard budget constraints and commercial goals for SEEs, and downsizing or closure of inefficient operations. Measures were also announced to raise the efficiency of tax collection, to reduce tax expenditure, to reform the bankrupt social security system, and to lower border protection and strengthen competition legislation.

Revised estimates for the 1994 consolidated budget indicate an overrun of around TL 30 trillion (0.7 per cent of GDP) compared with the April programme. Higher interest payments, partly because of greater reliance on domestic financing than envisaged,[21] accounted for around half of the additional deficit. The overshoot of the primary deficit target was modest (around 0.4 per cent of GDP), caused mainly by lower-than-expected revenues from privatisation. Slippage on items off the consolidated budget accounted for 0.5 per cent of GDP, reflecting small over-runs by SEEs and Extra-Budgetary Funds, but better outturns for municipalities. The 1994 budget deficit and PSBR were estimated in October at some 3.5 and 7.5 per cent of GDP, respectively, versus targets of 2.6 and 6.1 per cent.

The April measures underpinned a return of confidence in the financial system and a sharp flow back into the TL, with the ratio of TL deposits in M2Y rising from 42 per cent in April to a peak of 56 per cent in July[22] (Diagram 9). The exchange rate, which had fallen to more than TL 40 000 per US dollar in early April, recovered to TL 31 900 per dollar by the end of that month. Financial market stability was enhanced by the resumption of domestic Treasury borrowing at end-May. This was initially at exceptionally high rates of interest (50 per cent over three months), but permitted the debt financing of the PSBR and the repayment of some Central Bank advances. The rapid swing back to TL prompted a US$3.5 billion rebuilding of foreign reserves between early April and end-August – compared with a targeted increase of US$1 billion by the end of the year.

While the Central Bank regained the ability to control the money supply, the stance of monetary policy remained difficult to assess. With WPI inflation dropping below 2 per cent a month in the summer and optimism rising, interest rates on 3-month Treasury bills dropped to 22 per cent a quarter by the end of August (with a parallel drop in deposit rates). But the level of ''real'' interest rates is difficult to judge, as private-sector inflation expectations differ widely from official inflation forecasts. Capital inflows were not sufficiently sterilised, and broad money grew rapidly, especially in the summer. Moreover, the real depreciation of some 30 per cent (as measured by the Secretariat) is a large net stimulus to aggregate demand. The resurgence of inflation in September and October stopped the fall in interest rates, with quarterly yields on 3-month Treasury bills rising from a mid-October low of 19.4 per cent to 26.5 per cent by end-December. Nonetheless, continuing rapid growth of the monetary aggregates suggests that monetary conditions are not yet bearing down on inflation.

Policy requirements in the short run

An immediate policy requirement is to continue with budgetary consolidation efforts so as to restore a sustainable fiscal position as rapidly as possible. An indicator of the fiscal effort needed to attain a sustainable fiscal position is "the financeable budget balance" which is the level of the primary budget balance – the total deficit less debt interest payments – consistent with a given government debt-to-GDP ratio and a given inflation rate.[23] The "financeable balance" depends on the rate of GDP growth, the real interest rate and the desired ratio of base money to GDP. Annex II shows calculations suggesting that the "financeable balance" in Turkey may be one with a primary budget surplus of close to 2 per cent of GDP in the short-term, but declining in the medium-term as policy credibility is established. Failure to maintain a primary surplus would imply either a rising debt to GDP ratio and/or continued high inflation – with actual inflation outcomes depending on the extent of money financing of the total deficit.

The measures introduced in April 1994 are estimated to have achieved an approximate total primary budget balance in 1994, compared with a primary deficit of 6 per cent in 1993. A primary surplus of 1¼ per cent is targeted in the 1995 budget. If this target is attained, fiscal policy would be close to a sustainable path. However, this will not be an easy task. There are substantial pressures on the 1995 budget, the more so as inflation has not been quickly reined in, and interest rates are very high relative to official inflation forecasts (see below).

The 1995 budget envisages a consolidated budget deficit of TL 198 trillion, up TL 59 trillion from the estimated 1994 outcome, but down from 3.5 to 3.3 per cent of GDP (Table 10). Revenue as a share of GDP is expected to fall only slightly, in spite of the absence of one-off taxes as occurred in 1994, and a cyclically low 1994 tax base. Additional revenue is expected from the 1993 corporate tax reform and from improvements in tax administration (the latter expected to yield an additional TL 20 trillion in 1995). Unlike the 1994 programme, the 1995 budget excludes privatisation revenue, which is now assigned to covering the costs of closure and rationalisation of SEEs (*e.g.* redundancies, retraining and restructuring). However, the budget will benefit from privatisation in so far as subsidies to loss-making SEEs will be sharply reduced. In the event, additional tax and revenue measures were approved in early 1995 as part of a package to increase revenue.

Table 10. **1995 Draft budget estimates**

TL trillion

	1994 Original programme	1994 April programme	1994 Estimate	1995 Programme
Consolidated budget				
Revenues	627	782	770	1 133
Non-interest spending	601	597	607	943
Primary balance	26	185	163	190
Interest payments	218	288	302	388
Budget balance	−192	−103	−139	−198
Total public sector				
Non-consolidated budget balance	−112	−140	−156	−103
Total public sector budget balance	−304	−243	−295	−301
Memorandum items				
Consolidated budget deficit (% of GDP)	6.5	2.6	3.5	3.3
PSBR (% of GDP)	10.3	6.1	7.4	5.0

Source: State Planning Organisation, and OECD estimates.

Non-interest spending is to be kept under strict control. Employment will be reduced through attrition and tight controls on hiring. Wages for public-sector workers are to be restricted in 1995. By contrast, small real increases are foreseen for civil servants, following real cuts of some 26 per cent in 1994. Indeed, past wage agreements have led to an unusual wage structure, with civil servants earning considerably less than contract workers for equivalent work.[24] Some 34 000 contract workers were to have been converted to lower-paid civil service status, but this proposal was rejected by Parliament. Personnel expenditure is now set to increase in line with the revised official inflation forecast for 1995.

Interest payments were originally budgeted at TL 388 trillion in 1995 based on the assumption that interest rates would fall with lower inflation. But, with an upward revision to inflation, interest payments will be higher, the more so if inflation expectations do not adjust rapidly to official inflation forecasts or if risk premia on government debt are higher than projected.

The lower PSBR in 1995 will help reduce inflation. But much stronger controls over monetary financing of deficits than in the past, and enhanced competition, are also necessary. New legislation still allowed the government to finance 15 per cent of the change in budget appropriations through Central Bank advances in 1994, though these will be steadily reduced to 3 per cent by 1998.[25] The process of bearing down on inflation and of building policy credibility would be greatly enhanced by more rapid progress in reducing the Central Bank financing of the PSBR.

Strict observance of money-financing limits means that a greater proportion of the deficit must be financed by debt. In any transition period from money to debt financing there is inevitably strong upward pressure on interest rates. As noted above, the government regained access to domestic capital markets in May 1994 at phenomenal interest rates (50 per cent a quarter). Notwithstanding impressive subsequent falls, "real" interest rates based on official inflation targets remain very high.[26] Even so, interest rates may have to rise substantially from present levels, given the priority attached to reining in inflation. Higher interest rates are necessary both to curtail the excessive monetary growth in recent months and to help reverse some of the real depreciation of the Turkish lira.

The real exchange rate of the Turkish lira (as measured by the OECD) depreciated by some 30 per cent between the fourth quarter of 1993 and the third quarter of 1994. This provided a substantial stimulus to the traded goods sector, which has led the recovery in demand in the second half of 1994. The current account is projected to remain in surplus of around 2 per cent of GDP, even when the economy returns to trend output, if this real exchange rate is "locked in". As Turkey should normally be a net importer of capital in the medium term, there is thus scope in principle to "trade off" some real appreciation for more rapid disinflation.[27]

The nominal exchange rate depreciated by 3 to 4 per cent a month between August and December 1994. If the rate of depreciation could be reduced to 1 per cent a month, underlying wholesale-price inflation could be reduced by around 1/2 percentage point a month. The higher interest rates necessary to achieve this would also enable the authorities to rein in money supply growth. OECD Secretariat estimates suggest that money supply growth of around 1 per cent a month combined with holding nominal exchange rate depreciation to 1 per cent a month would be needed to meet the official forecast of bringing the 12-month inflation rate below 40 per cent by the end of 1995.

As a higher real exchange rate further damps inflationary pressure (albeit by lowering competitiveness from its strong current position), it would facilitate fresh foreign borrowing. So long as this process is not exaggerated (as in the late 1980s), limited foreign borrowing would provide a respite to public sector crowding out on domestic capital markets – and help in lengthening the extremely short maturity structure of domestic government debt (currently only four months).

Higher interest rates would, no doubt, put temporary pressure on the PSBR. But a temporary rise in the PSBR would be well worth the price for reining in inflation – the more so as the risk of a debt explosion is limited. In this context, the most relevant criterion for fiscal consolidation is the primary budget balance. Once fiscal consolidation and lower inflation are on track, risk premia on government debt can be expected to be progressively, but decisively reduced.

Medium-term requirements

Beyond 1995 the primary goal of economic policy should be to consolidate the progress made on both the fiscal and inflation fronts and, where possible, to make further progress. Attainment of these goals would be facilitated by an explicit medium-term policy framework and policy rules. The Turkish government has traditionally prepared five-year plans, and the plan under preparation will be delayed by one year. In the past, these plans often lost policy relevance quickly, as they were rapidly overtaken by events. The next five-year plan provides an opportunity to put a credible medium-term policy framework in place. A number of key ingredients for such a framework, drawing on the experience of other OECD countries, is sketched out below.

The first element is explicit fiscal-policy goals. Many European countries are striving to meet the Maastricht criteria for the ratio of public debt to GDP and the general government deficit/GDP ratios. Some countries are aiming at eliminating structural budget deficits – deficits adjusted for the effects of business cycles – altogether. A few are aiming for actual budget balance. While there is no consensus as to what particular levels of public debt are best for any given country, there is broad agreement that there is a strong tendency for these to rise, as higher public spending often benefits selected interest groups with significant political influence. Setting explicit deficit and/or debt targets is a first step in fighting such a tendency. In the case of Turkey the current domestic debt-to-GDP ratio is low and the high foreign debt-to-GDP ratio should be attenuated by "real appreciation" of the lira. The OECD Secretariat's medium-term scenario suggests that in the year 2000 (when the economy is projected to re-attain trend output) the PSBR could still be around 4 per cent of GDP. This level of the PSBR would be consistent with a stable debt/GDP ratio of around 40 per cent because of high potential output growth in Turkey. It would be prudent, however, to aim at smaller structural deficits to provide the authorities with a safety margin.

The second requirement is to build in mechanisms which further the attainment of fiscal goals. In the United States, for example, the pay-as-you-go provision in the 1990 and 1993 budget laws require that any new government programme or tax cuts be financed through either spending cuts elsewhere or new revenue measures. Sequestration – across-the-board spending cuts in the case of failure to attain the targeted deficit – is another example of an enforcement mechanism. In the case of Turkey the minimum requirement would be to restrict the use of supplementary budgets to additional spending necessitated by such events as natural disasters. Such enforcement mechanisms would enhance the credibility of the authorities' commitment to fiscal goals.

The third need is for clear priorities among spending programmes. This will become all the more important as fiscal consolidation progresses and the total budget envelope is reduced. As discussed in Chapter III there is a strong case for higher spending on human resource development, notably in the areas of education and health care. The experience of the high-performing Asian economies (HPAEs) shows that the priority attached in these countries to human capital development[28] has contributed not only to raising potential growth, but also to spreading the benefits of growth among the population and maintaining a social consensus.

Fourth, it is essential to accompany fiscal consolidation with structural reforms that eliminate wasteful government spending and improve the efficiency of government programmes in achieving socio-economic goals. As noted in Chapter III, the scope for improvement in these areas is vast and could in itself virtually eliminate the PSBR. Indeed, this is the only way that fiscal consolidation can be sustained in the medium term without leading to unacceptable socio-political tensions.

Last, but not least, it is of critical importance to set up a distinctly anti-inflationary monetary policy, which has long been inhibited by irresponsible fiscal management. The progressive programmed reduction in the Treasury's reliance on Central Bank financing should pave the way towards an adoption of a new monetary policy framework.

Specific institutional arrangements for monetary policy differ across OECD countries, but most of them have adopted some sort of nominal anchor to influence inflation expectations. For Turkey one option would be to peg its exchange rate to a key currency of a low inflation country (*e.g.* the Deutschemark) or to a basket of currencies (as is done by Iceland). But this can be a high risk option, if inflation remains high and private-sector price expectations continue to be strongly backward looking. Another option would be to continue with a floating exchange rate, but to have an explicit and progressively lower inflation target and to steer the course of monetary policy accordingly (as in New Zealand, Canada and the United Kingdom). In practice, this would be akin to a sliding exchange-rate target with wide bands – the floors being calibrated in line with official inflation targets – with a clear commitment to defend these floors. Such an option has all the advantages and disadvantages of an adjustable peg system. But until fiscal sustainability is "on track", a rigid nominal anchor policy would seem to be ruled out, while some nominal anchor is nonetheless needed to influence price expectations.[29]

III. Structural reform to underpin continued economic progress

Following a severe foreign debt crisis in 1978-79, Turkey in early 1980 launched a far-reaching stabilisation programme based on structural reforms. These reforms represented a sea change in orientation, shifting Turkey from an inward to a more outward-looking economy based on free-market principles. Measures included: the abolition of rigid foreign-exchange and capital controls; deregulation of financial markets; unilateral cuts in border protection; and the encouragement of exports and foreign investment. The tax system was also reformed and a value-added tax introduced. Efforts to enhance the efficiency of State economic enterprises (SEEs) were strengthened and the ground laid for their privatisation.

Reforms in the early 1980s (especially lower border protection) provided the base for Turkey's good record on exports and economic growth. But the reforms were partial. Despite a promising start, the pace of reform waned in the latter half of the 1980s. A new impetus here is clearly needed, and indeed supply-side reform features prominently in the April 1994 programme's agenda. A number of initiatives have been taken. The public sector is acknowledged as being too large and inefficient and, hence, a major drag on economic growth. Proposed initiatives include: imposing hard budget constraints on loss-making SEEs; privatisation; raising the efficiency of core public-sector activities; improving the efficiency and equity of the tax system; reform of the bankrupt social security system; establishing a social safety net; and reform of competition policy. Rapid progress in these areas is essential if the economy is to cope with intensified competition in the wake of the entry into the EU customs union scheduled for end-1995, as well as to free the resources needed to boost private investment, job creation and to upgrade Turkey's social services, human capital and infrastructure. This chapter discusses a number of reform areas which affect the efficiency of the public sector, government efforts to enhance competitive pressures operating on the economy and the state of human resource development in Turkey.

Rationalising public-sector operations

Reform of SEEs

SEEs were originally created to play a leading role in investment, employment and economic growth. With the benefit of hindsight, however, they have imposed a heavy deadweight burden on the private sector. In 1993, the output of SEEs accounted for around 10 per cent of GDP,[30] but the deficits of non-financial SEEs represented 3.6 per cent of GDP, even after central government transfers of almost 1.5 per cent of GDP.[31] SEEs' debt burdens are very high.[32]

Experience in the United Kingdom, New Zealand, Australia and other OECD countries since the 1980s[33] is indicative of the large productivity gains and savings possible through restructuring of SEEs. Key to success is the replacement of non-economic incentives by rational cost and price structures and commercial goals. Reform has been slow in Turkey, due to the vocal opposition of special interest groups and a weak social-political consensus. Some progress has been made in imposing hard budget constraints. Management attitudes are also changing due to the imposition of financing limits (as part of the IMF stand-by's performance guidelines), a freeze on hiring and investment, and the lifting of the ban on the sequestration of SEE assets due to non-payment.

The potential efficiency gains of SEE reform are large. No official estimates of potential efficiency gains exist, but these may be approximated by the 30 to 40 per cent gap in value-added per worker between public-sector and private firms. Value-added per unit of fixed capital in private firms may be three times higher than in SEEs (see Table 11). If reform raised labour and capital productivity in SEEs to levels comparable with private firms, the level of GDP would be raised by 6 to 8 per cent (see Table 12). These are lower-range estimates limited to static gains. Dynamic efficiency gains through enhanced competition and better quality investment could tend to boost TFP further.[34]

A major factor inhibiting a better productivity performance of SEEs is the lack of product market competition. Industry concentration is very high; there is as yet no formal competition policy; and although border protection is being

Table 11. **Labour and capital productivity**

	Real net value added/number of employees (TL million)			Real net value added/real fixed assets (percentage)		
	Total	Public	Private	Total	Public	Private
1982	31.7	24.8	39.3			
1983	25.3	17.3	36.0	0.626	0.406	0.969
1984	28.7	21.6	37.4	0.695	0.485	0.992
1985	30.4	25.4	36.4	0.442	0.276	0.933
1986	33.0	24.4	44.1	0.448	0.247	1.046
1987	42.5	34.3	51.8	0.514	0.303	1.152
1988	41.1	36.6	47.1	0.507	0.332	1.096
1989	39.9	35.2	46.2	0.502	0.325	1.049
1990	41.6	32.5	52.1	0.499	0.287	1.063
1991	42.4	26.6	61.9	0.489	0.243	1.007
1992	50.5	33.2	72.0	0.544	0.290	1.070
Average	37.0	28.4	47.7	0.527	0.319	1.038
Average (1985-92)	40.2	31.0	51.4	0.493	0.288	1.052

Source: Özmucur, S., "Financial Indicators, Profitability and Productivity in the Major 500 Concerns, 1980 and 1992", *Journal of the Istanbul Chamber of Commerce*, September 1993.

lowered unilaterally, it remains high. Apart from this, the reasons for poor productivity performance of SEEs are generic:

- the lack of independent management;
- pursuit of non-commercial goals;
- the absence of hard budget constraints.

Present institutional arrangements foster economic rent seeking rather than wealth creation. In the past, SEEs often "absorbed" excess labour, and investment decisions were strongly influenced by non-economic factors (at negative real rates of interest). The legacy of these policies is stark: wage costs and debt service per unit of sales in 1992 were double those in private firms, worsening from 1989.[35] As SEEs are highly unionised and are wage-leaders (wage levels are often double those in the private sector for comparable jobs), wage increases in excess of productivity gains were routinely granted, with no risk of insolvency. The absence of hard budget constraints on SEEs has been a major factor for chronic large PSBRs and high inflation.

SEEs reform is a central plank of the government's structural programme. The Treasury is monitoring the deficits of the seven largest loss-making SEEs

Table 12. Total factor productivity

	Share of wages and salaries in net value added			Number of employees Percentage changes			Real fixed assets Percentage changes		
	Total	Public	Private	Total	Public	Private	Total	Public	Private
1981	..	..	..	-3.5	-6.9	1.4	..	..	..
1982	52.6	66.4	42.3	-1.6	-7.8	6.6	..	..	..
1983	55.5	74.9	42.7	22.5	33.0	10.6	..	..	..
1984	46.4	57.5	38.2	-4.6	8.8	1.1	-2.5	-4.5	2.5
1985	40.4	41.3	39.4	8.1	13.5	1.5	79.8	134.7	5.0
1986	37.9	44.3	32.6	2.1	0.4	4.5	9.4	7.8	12.9
1987	34.4	40.5	29.4	1.1	2.6	5.9	13.4	11.2	13.1
1988	33.5	35.4	31.8	5.3	6.2	4.1	3.3	3.5	-0.5
1989	46.6	55.5	39.1	2.0	0.3	4.2	0.2	-1.6	6.7
1990	59.9	76.0	48.5	-1.8	-3.9	0.7	2.8	0.7	12.0
1991	82.3	130.4	55.8	-3.2	-1.2	-5.5	0.8	-4.6	18.5
1992	75.0	117.5	50.3	-4.3	-3.5	-5.4	2.3	1.1	3.6
Average	51.3	67.2	40.9	1.8	1.6	2.5	12.2	16.5	8.2
Average (1985-92)	51.3	67.6	40.9	1.2	1.2	1.3	14.0	19.1	8.9

	Real net value added Percentage changes			Weighted factor inputs Percentage changes			Total factor productivity Percentage changes		
	Total	Public	Private	Total	Public	Private	Total	Public	Private
1983	-2.1	-7.2	1.4	12.2	23.3	4.5	-14.3	-30.5	-3.1
1984	8.4	14.0	4.9	-3.6	-7.3	1.9	11.9	21.3	3.0
1985	14.4	33.4	-1.3	48.7	74.8	3.6	-34.3	-41.4	-4.9
1986	10.8	-3.5	26.6	6.6	4.6	9.9	4.2	-8.1	16.7
1987	30.2	36.5	24.5	8.9	5.3	10.9	21.3	31.2	13.7
1988	1.9	13.3	-5.3	4.0	4.5	0.9	-2.1	8.8	-6.2
1989	-0.9	-3.5	2.1	1.0	-0.7	5.8	-1.8	-2.8	-3.7
1990	2.3	-11.3	13.5	0.4	-2.3	7.1	2.0	-9.0	6.5
1991	-1.4	-19.0	12.2	-2.0	-1.1	6.0	0.7	-17.9	6.2
1992	14.0	20.5	10.1	-2.9	-4.6	-1.1	16.9	25.1	11.3
Average	7.8	7.3	8.9	7.3	9.7	4.9	0.5	-2.3	3.9
Average (1985-92)	8.9	8.3	10.3	8.1	10.1	5.4	0.9	-1.8	4.9

Source: See Table 11.

(95 per cent of SEEs deficit), as part of the performance criteria in the IMF stand-by arrangement.[36] Starting in 1994, SEEs have been subject to commercial law and will be expected to operate according to market principles. Those SEEs which are identified as burdens are being downsized, rehabilitated or will be liquidated. Labour shedding and closure feasibility studies are being speeded.[37] SEEs that cannot be privatised will be closed and their assets sold.[38] These reforms, if realised, would generate the most significant efficiency improvements in a decade.[39]

In 1994, the ban on the attachment and liquidation of SEEs' (and municipalities') assets in response to tax or commercial arrears was lifted (in May and October respectively). Commercial banks have subsequently blocked the accounts of some loss-making SEEs and other assets (cars and buildings) have been sequestered. Sequestration has had a salutary effect on SEEs management attitudes. It will reinforce budget constraints and facilitate the closure or divestiture of non-viable SEEs. Efforts to speed the use of private sector management practices (*e.g.* outsourcing of commercial services, private-sector water billing and collection,[40] catering, cleaning, etc.) are being made in SEEs. Some of these practices are also being introduced into core public-sector activities.

Speeding privatisation

The second plank to streamlining the public sector is to accelerate privatisation. From its inception in 1986, the privatisation programme has been plagued by legal and political obstacles, with revenue as of September 1994 totalling only $2.76 billion.[41] Outright asset sales have been slow, due to the small size of domestic capital markets, which has necessitated block sales and foreign participation.[42] Firms ready for privatisation (without further restructuring) were placed under the supervision of the Public Participation Administration (PPA) in 1993. Other SEEs remain under Treasury supervision.

The 1994 stabilisation package announced an ambitious privatisation programme, with revenue originally planned at more than $3 billion for 1994. Streamlined legislation was passed quickly by Parliament. In the event, the act allowing privatisation by decree (*via* a high level board decision without further Parliamentary referral) was annulled by the Constitutional Court. Several earlier enabling acts were also annulled. These delays have lowered expected revenue in 1994 to around $0.8 billion.[43] Revised legislation, which includes additional provisions governing early retirement and redundancy payments was passed in November. A new agency, the Privatisation Administration (OIB) will handle the sales (of some US$60 billion of total assets) and aims to raise US$5 billion gross in 1995.[44] Sales will require the unanimous approval of the High Board of Privatisation, comprising the Prime Minister and four other ministers.[45]

The on-going nature of privatisation and restructuring of SEEs will be supported by a social safety net, which is a feature of the revised privatisation bill approved by Parliament. Studies are well advanced on setting up a self-financing, unemployment compensation scheme funded by employee/employer contributions with technical aid from the World Bank. A pilot system was scheduled to start before end-1994, with the intention of being operational by 1997. The advantages of this approach may be visible over the medium term. However, the establishment of such a system must strike a balance between providing an essential insurance function, while not setting the net so high as to impose excessive non-wage labour costs and hiring disincentives. In the interim, redundancy payments serve as compensation for job losses from privatisation and rationalisation of the public sector. In addition, retraining and placement of displaced workers, which will draw on privatisation funds, are to be stepped up as a means of speeding restructuring.

Streamlining agricultural support systems

SEEs in the agri-food sector accounted for almost 60 per cent of total SEE borrowing requirements in 1993, a large part of which was due to agricultural support policies.[46] Since late 1993, the government has issued several decrees aimed at shifting the system of intervention purchases towards deficiency payments (cotton in September 1993, tobacco in 1994). Special *ad valorem* taxes that had applied to many tariff lines including agricultural commodities were also abolished in anticipation of the Customs Union with the EC, as was the tariff on fertiliser. These changes improved transparency but did not lower the average level of border protection significantly.[47]

The level of total assistance to agriculture – as measured by producer subsidy equivalent (PSE) – rose from an average of 16 per cent in 1970-86 to 29 per cent in 1987-90 and to 39 per cent in 1991-93 as a result of increases in both the number of products covered by price support and generosity of assistance. Turkey's PSE at 35 per cent in 1993 was below the OECD average (43 per cent), but significantly higher than in major agricultural producers such as Canada, Australia, New Zealand and the United States.[48] In 1994, the PSE dropped significantly to 10 per cent (joint second lowest in the OECD) owing to rising world prices, the large depreciation of the Turkish lira and, to a lesser extent, cuts in subsidies.

The shift to a more market-oriented agricultural system was confirmed in April 1994: government support purchases were limited to cereals, sugarbeet and tobacco, and support price adjustments limited in line with policies for wages and prices. As in most countries, price supports tend to favour a limited number of specialised, commercial farmers who often are relatively wealthy. Further, as basic food represents 36 per cent of household spending in the CPI (and a larger proportion for low-income groups), price support systems may aggravate the unevenness of Turkey's income distribution.[49] For these reasons, agricultural policy is to shift its emphasis from price support to specific subsidies for production inputs,[50] provision of credit facilities and direct payments to a targeted population. Agricultural subsidies have been lowered substantially in 1994 and are programmed to continue at these lower levels in the 1995 budget.[51]

Social security

Unlike most countries with immature contributory social security systems the Turkish system is a major drain on the budget. This reflects excessively early pension entitlement, inadequate contribution levels and poor collection rates. The Sixth Plan targeted 67 per cent of total population to be covered by social security (health, invalidity and pensions) whereas the outcome was 74 per cent in 1991.

Women and men can retire after 20 and 25 years of service, respectively. These work-life obligations are barely one-half those in most OECD countries and allow people to retire and draw benefit in their early 40s.[52] The present system provides a disincentive to work and is actuarially insolvent.

The financial positions of the social security (SSK) and BAG-KUR (social insurance institution of craftsmen, tradesmen and other self-employed) are untenable. Late collection of premiums (due to high inflation and low penalties) and a rapidly rising ratio of inactive versus active insured workers have led to a financing crisis. The SSK has sold all its financial and some of its physical assets to meet current commitments, and is receiving transfers from the Treasury.

Collection rates for the SSK are reported to be around 70 per cent, due partly to large SEEs and municipal government arrears. Collection rates of the BAG-KUR are even worse. They are reported to be only 10 per cent, due to ineffective administration and the practice of paying arrears immediately before retirement with negligible penalties.

Measures have been taken to increase rents charged on property owned by SSK institutions, to widen the wage base and the number of contributors among public employees and the self-employed, and to accelerate premium collections *via* tighter control and auditing. Arrears of the municipalities will be deducted from their budgetary allocations. But any viable solution will need radical increases in retirement age and higher contribution rates.[53]

A draft bill to raise the minimum BAG-KUR retirement age and premiums has been submitted to Parliament for discussion and approval. A draft bill on reform of the SSK is also under preparation, with technical aid from the World Bank. The intention is to gradually reduce present invalidity and pension entitlements and to raise retirement age (initially to 55 years for women and 60 years for men). Private health insurance and the establishment of fully-funded private pension funds are also being encouraged.

Tax reform

OECD data show that in 1992, total Turkish tax revenue (excluding social security) was 18.4 per cent of GDP – 10 percentage points below the OECD average, and the lowest among OECD countries.[54] Turkey's limited tax capacity makes it difficult to finance government expenditure. The tax base is small because significant sectors of the economy, SEEs and small farmers, pay virtually no tax (apart from a 2 to 4 per cent withholding tax on agricultural deliveries). Progress has been made in reducing tax exemptions (cuts in corporate tax exemptions, investment incentives, VAT and customs duty rebates), but tax expenditure remains pervasive. Tax administration is still inadequate in the face of widespread under-reporting and a large underground economy.

Reform of the tax system started in 1981, with few changes in its basic characteristics being made over the past several years. The personal tax base is small, as dependent employees represent roughly one-quarter of total employment. The corporate tax base is similarly limited, given the weight of SEEs. Direct tax incidence is thus capricious and uneven. For dependent employees who cannot shelter their income, tax burdens are high by OECD standards[55] (see Diagram 12). High inflation, lenient tax penalties and frequent tax amnesties fail to discourage late payment or under-reporting, so the government typically loses up to a quarter of its "real" tax revenue due to poor or late collection. These shortcomings are being addressed (see below).

Against this background, heavy reliance is placed on indirect and *ad hoc* taxes, which together accounted for more than one-half of tax revenue in 1993. This share will rise further as the full impact of higher value-added tax (VAT) rates in November 1993 and the elimination of VAT rebates to those in employment (equivalent to 1 per cent of GDP) take effect.[56] Given the importance of the underground economy, VAT is a relatively effective way of raising revenue.[57] The phasing out of *ad hoc* foreign trade taxes,[58] in preparation for EU customs union, will result in substantial revenue losses. Draft legislation is in Parliament to replace this revenue through a special consumption tax on luxury items.

At the end of 1993, simplifications to the tax system were made as well as improvements in its administration.[59] For corporate income tax, statutory rates were reduced from 46 to 25 per cent, while a minimum effective rate of 20 per

Diagram 12. **AVERAGE RATE OF INCOME TAX IN 1991**
Paid by a production worker in the manufacturing sector

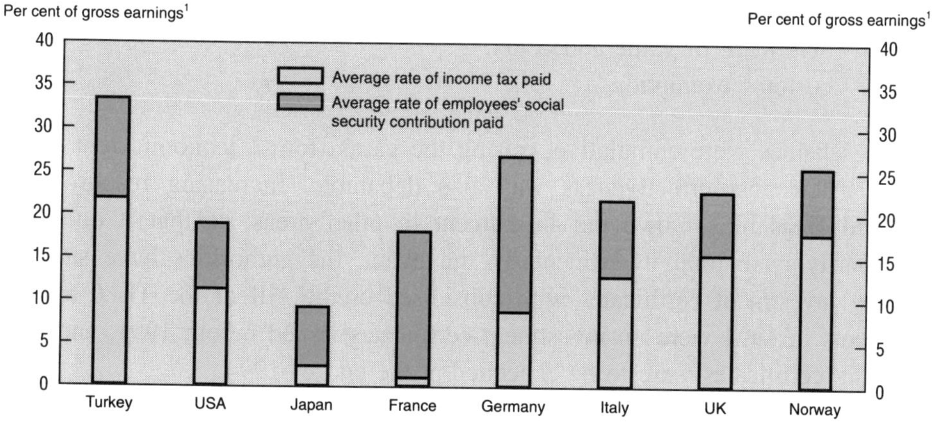

Per cent of gross earnings[1]

Per cent of gross earnings[1]

Average rate of income tax paid
Average rate of employees' social security contribution paid

Turkey USA Japan France Germany Italy UK Norway

1. One-earner couple with two children.
Source: OECD, *The Tax/Benefit Position of Production Workers.*

43

cent was introduced for all corporate tax payers. Most of the tax exemptions for corporate tax were abolished. Personal income tax brackets were also raised to avoid bracket creep, and rates of advance payment of future tax obligation substantially increased.[60] A larger proportion of individuals are being shifted from the lump-sum into the income tax system, and the standard of living criteria for tax assessment for the self-employed are being adjusted.

One goal of tax reform is to establish a "level playing field" to improve decision-making and resource allocation. Further progress is needed in this area. Despite unilateral cuts in border protection, the dispersion of tariff rates remains pronounced. Furthermore, the use of subsidised credit is extensive and not targeted. Resource allocation decisions may also be distorted by tax shelters, industry or regional tax concessions and wide variance in sector-specific tariff rates. Official estimates of tax expenditure are not available, but it would appear to be large, albeit diminishing.

A number of industrial investment incentives are in place, but are being phased out for end-1994. Investment certificates originally provided allowances ranging from 30 to 100 per cent according to region and sector (recently cut to 20 and 70 per cent, respectively).[61] Such schemes included:

- investment allowances;
- exemption of tax, duty and social charges;
- investment financing fund;
- building and construction charges exemption;
- deferment of value added tax;
- customs exemption.

These schemes were cumulative, raising the gains from "economic rent seeking". Their cost effectiveness was also debatable. Increasing resources to targeted areas may crowd out investment in other areas, so that it does not necessarily raise total investment. In the event, the authorities have stopped issuing investment certificates with subsidised credit. All of the TL 6 trillion payments in 1994 were on investment certificates issued before 1991, and outstanding certificates were to be cancelled at the end of 1994.

In summary, the tax system has most of the attributes of a modern tax regime. But its administration is under-funded and inadequate, in part owing to the perverse effects of high inflation.[62] Greater resources are to be provided to improve tax administration and a tax investigation unit will be set up. In view of radical changes in recent years, raising tax rates[63] is a second-best solution to base broadening *via* a cut-back in tax expenditure and more effective administration. However, it is unclear whether base broadening alone will be sufficient to meet the budget's revenue targets.

Enhancing competitive forces

Lowering border protection

Preparation for customs union with the EU by end-1995 is a key policy parameter and will have potent supply-side effects on the Turkish economy. In the absence of active domestic competition, free trade (or a customs union) will impose a powerful element of competitive discipline on the economy. The challenge is to make a smooth transition at minimum cost.

Customs union (albeit a second-best solution to free trade) is an efficient means of heightening competition and productivity, so long as trade diversion is small and adjustment to the new policy regime is rapid. To date, the private sector has demonstrated impressive flexibility. No sector-specific waivers have been asked for in the phasing out of tariffs on imports from the EC/EFTA, while some Turkish exports remain subject to voluntary restraints.[64] As regards the public sector, customs union may also help to build a consensus for faster structural reform, as well as imposing constraints on macroeconomic policy.

Turkey began the process of unilateral tariff reduction in December 1983, when average (nominal) tariffs on a trade-weighted basis were cut from nearly 40 to 22 per cent. Under the trade regime for 1993, there are two tariff rates: the EC/EFTA rate, for imports from these zones, and the most-favoured-nations (MFN) rate for imports from other areas. The simple average MFN rate for all imports was 9.5 per cent and that for the EC/EFTA 5.0 per cent (Table 13), giving a weighted average of around 7 per cent (falling 10 per cent in 1994 and a further 5 to 10 per cent in 1995). Turkey applies no tariff quotas and does not maintain any variable levies.

EC/EFTA tariffs are scheduled to be completely phased out by end-1995. The 3 to 5 per cent drop in nominal tariff rates will be small. However, remaining protection will be high, until the Mass Housing Fund (MHF) levy which applied

Table 13. **Tariff treatment for imports into Turkey, 1993**

	MFN[1] rates	EC/EFTA rates	Mass housing fund
Average	9.5	5.0	17.1[2]
Standard deviation	5.7	4.9	10.6
Coefficient of variation	60.0	98.0	62.0
By degrees of processing			
Primary products	6.5	4.8	19.7
Semi-processed goods	8.5	3.8	16.5
Finished goods	10.8	5.9	16.9
By sector			
Agriculture	7.1	6.0	21.2
Mining	5.1	2.4	16.1
Industry	9.7	5.0	16.9

Note: The standard deviation measures the absolute dispersion or variability of a distribution; the coefficient of variation is a measure of relative dispersion, defined as the standard deviation divided by the mean and expressed in percentage terms.
1. Most favoured nation.
2. The average is calculated only on the tariff lines which carry ad valorem rates.
Source: GATT Secretariat based on 1993 Import regime.

to 13 400 tariff lines in 1994 (Table 13) is completely phased out.[65] The MHF levy raises nominal protection to nearly 27 per cent on MFN imports, but is scheduled to be phased out in 1995, starting with 20 per cent cuts on 1 January (subsequently delayed to March) and 1 July, and to be totally eliminated by end-1995.

Effective rates of protection are difficult to estimate and can vary depending on methodology.[66] However, it is clear that border protection has been brought down steadily, but remains relatively high. Customs union and the phasing out of the MHF will lower protection significantly. Notwithstanding this progress, a continuing concern is the large coefficient of variation of protection, which introduces large tax wedges between industries and products.

Finally, Turkey has an array of export subsidies and duty exemptions which will have to be phased out with customs union, as well as under GATT rules. This will in principle affect the discount on electricity consumed in the manufacture of goods for export, transport premiums and import duty remission schemes.[67]

Strengthening competition policy

An ongoing constraint in lowering inflation is the lack of competition and high domestic industry concentration.[68] This would not be a problem if active foreign competition was present (see above). But border protection is still quite high. Turkey was until recently among the few OECD countries which did not have an anti-cartel law. In addition, competitive tendering for government procurement is not systematic. In early December, Parliament unanimously approved the anti-cartel bill, along with a series of other bills (including one covering intellectual property rights) aimed at achieving legislative harmony with the EU. Consumer protection legislation is also before Parliament, and a Competition Board will be established for this purpose.

Human resource development

Experience in the High-Performing Asian Economies (HPAEs) is that structural reform is essential as it releases resources that can be used to raise basic education and health services – thereby improving income distribution and helping to build a social consensus. These elements are weak, albeit improving significantly, in Turkey. In 1993, the subsidies received and deficits run by the SEEs exceeded spending on either health or education.

There is no simple or comprehensive measure of human resource development. A useful, albeit simple summary measure is the UN human development index (HDI) based on literacy (mean years of schooling), life expectancy and real per capita GDP. On the HDI measure, Turkey was among the top ten countries in terms of improvement over the period 1960-92, leaving the ranks of the low and entering the ranks of the medium level countries.

By 1992, Turkey ranked 68th (71st in 1990) among 173 countries.[69] This improvement in ranking was due to above-average economic performance, as Turkey lags in health and education outcomes. A particular feature is the wide east/west and urban/rural disparities in health and education standards.[70] The challenge is to reduce these disparities rapidly.

Life expectancy

Life expectancy at birth rose from 48.3 to 66.7 years between 1960 and 1990, while infant death rates dropped from 206 to 58 per thousand over the same period. The figure for life expectancy is low by OECD standards, but similar to those for other Middle-East countries, the Philippines and Brazil (life expectancies of 64 and 66 years, respectively).

In the majority of low and middle-income countries, there is a strong negative correlation between literacy rates (of women) and birth rates. In Turkey, more educated women desire fewer children and are more likely to achieve their family planning goals (Table 14), although the reasons for this are numerous.[71]

Table 14. **Number of children by educational level of women** [1]

As a percentage of the category

Number of children		Total		Illiterate		Literate without diploma		Literate	
		Desired [2]	Actual	Desired [2]	Actual	Desired [2]	Actual	Desired [2]	Actual
0	Less than desired	0.6	7.5	0.9	4.3	0.7	3.4	0.5	9.5
1		4.3	11.3	2.7	4.3	2.9	5.7	5.3	15.8
2		54.9	18.4	39.5	7.4	51.8	12.9	64.9	25.7
3		24.4	15.1	28.8	10.6	28.8	15.2	21.4	18.1
4	More than desired	7.8	12.0	14.0	12.2	8.3	17.2	3.8	12.0
5		3.1	9.6	6.1	13.2	2.7	13.4	1.2	7.2
6		1.2	7.5	2.4	12.0	1.0	11.0	0.3	4.5
7+		1.1	18.6	2.5	36.0	0.8	21.2	0.3	7.2

Number of children		Primary school		Lower secondary		Upper secondary		Higher education	
		Desired [2]	Actual	Desired [2]	Actual	Desired [2]	Actual	Desired [2]	Actual
0	Less than desired	0.4	10.0	0.6	11.3	0.3	14.9	0.4	15.9
1		4.8	14.9	6.2	24.0	10.7	31.8	12.8	34.2
2		64.8	25.5	79.2	38.0	77.6	40.4	78.1	38.4
3		22.6	20.1	11.2	16.8	8.6	10.0	7.0	9.8
4	More than desired	3.5	12.8	1.2	6.6	0.6	1.7	0.4	1.5
5		1.1	7.2	0.2	2.1	0.3	0.9	0.2	0.0
6		0.3	4.0	0.0	0.9	0.0	0.1	0.0	0.2
7+		0.2	5.5	0.2	0.3	0.0	0.2	0.0	0.0

1. On average: 5 years of education for primary, 8 for lower secondary, 11 for upper secondary.
2. Equal 100 by adding those with no opinion.
Source: State Institute of Statistics, *Turkish Demographic Survey*, 1989.

Against this background, Turkey's population growth slowed in the 1960s and 1970s, but stabilised in the 1980s, due to rapidly falling death rates (from high levels). Population growth between 1990 and 1995 is estimated at 1.9 per cent per annum, resulting in a relatively young average age. In 1990, 35.8 per cent of the population was aged under 15 and only 4.2 per cent 65 years or over (Table 15 and Diagram 13). The urban population is growing rapidly (around 5 per cent a year) with very rapid growth in small and medium-sized cities especially in the Eastern provinces.

Literacy

Literacy has risen dramatically over the past 20 years and the wide male/female literacy gap has significantly narrowed (Table 16). Given current policies, illiteracy is a stock rather than a flow problem, which explains Turkey's comparatively low ranking on this criterion.[72] Plans to raise compulsory education from 5 to 8 years and to improve curriculum and school facilities are under consideration with the aid of the World Bank.

Youth enrolment rates have risen dramatically over the past 20 years. In 1991, virtually all of the age group corresponding to primary education were

Table 15. **Demographic trends in Turkey**

	1960	1970	1980	1990	1991	1992	1993
Population (million)[1]	27.8	35.6	44.7	56.5	57.3	58.4	59.5
Annual average growth (per cent)[2]	2.9	2.5	2.3	2.2	1.9	1.9	1.9
Share of urban population (per cent)[3]	27.1	32.4	42.1	54.0	55.0	56.2	57.6
Growth of urban population (per cent)	4.8	4.6	4.4	5.0	4.4	3.9	4.5
Growth of rural population (per cent)	2.3	1.7	0.6	–0.8	–0.9	–0.6	–1.6
Life expectancy at birth (years)[4]	48.3	55.1	61.5	66.7	66.9	67.2	67.4
Infant mortality (per cent of live birth)[4]	20.6	15.8	11.1	5.8	5.5	5.2	4.9
Birth rate[4]	4.7	3.9	3.2	2.5	2.4	2.4	2.3
Death rate[4]	2.0	1.4	1.0	0.7	0.7	0.7	0.7

1. Figures for 1960, 1970, 1980 and 1990 are the results of Population Censuses. Figures for 1991, 1992, and 1993 are mid-year population estimates which are based on Seventh Five Year Development Plan studies.
2. Figures for 1960, 1970 and 1980 are the annual averages for the preceding 10 year period.
3. Urban population is the population of localities with 20 000 and more inhabitants.
4. The figures appearing under the 1960, 1970 and 1980 columns relate the 1955-60, 1965-70 and 1975-80 periods respectively. The following figures indicate annual rates.
Source: State Institute of Statistics, State Planning Organisation.

Diagram 13. **AGE PYRAMIDS OF POPULATION**

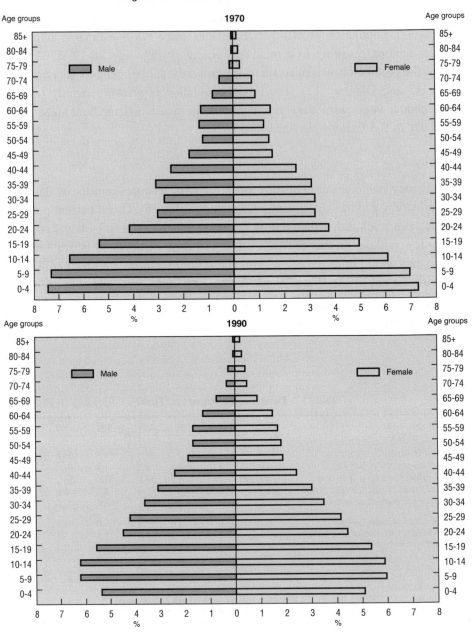

Source: State Institute of Statistics, *Statistical Indicators, 1923-1992.*

Table 16. **Population by literacy, education levels and sex**

	Male			Female		
	1970	1980	1990	1970	1980	1990
Literate	70.3	79.9	88.8	41.8	54.6	72.0
Literate without diploma	24.5	18.4	16.3	16.6	14.6	15.6
Primary school (6-11 years old)	36.1	44.2	49.1	20.7	31.4	43.1
Junior high school (12-14 years old)	4.9	7.6	9.6	2.2	3.7	5.4
High school (15-18 years old)	3.4	6.4	9.5	1.8	3.7	6.0
Higher education	1.3	3.3	4.2	0.6	1.2	1.8

Source: State Institute of Statistics, *Statistical Yearbook of Turkey,* 1993.

enrolled. However, enrolment drops off quickly after the lower secondary level, with strong emphasis on vocational as opposed to general education. In 1991, the youth (aged 5 to 29 years) to total population ratio – 50 per cent – was the highest among OECD countries. But the student to total population ratio was slightly below the OECD average (Table 17, columns 2-5).

Resources allocated to public education in Turkey have risen steadily, reaching 4 per cent of GDP in 1991, compared with an OECD average of 5.2 per cent[73]

Table 17. **Youth population and participation in education, 1991**

	Population, 5-29 years as per cent of total population	Share of enrolled students in the population, 5-29 years				Students as a share of total population
		Total	Primary and lower secondary	Upper secondary	Tertiary education[1]	
Turkey	**51.8**[2]	**38.8**	**31.0**	**5.3**	**2.5**	**20.1**
France	35.8	57.7	35.8	12.3	9.6	20.7
Germany	32.4	50.0	29.0	12.4	8.6	16.2
Ireland	43.1	56.9	40.7	10.3	5.8	24.5
Portugal	44.4	47.0	34.0	9.1	4.0	20.9
Spain	39.1	57.3	32.0	17.0	8.3	22.4
United Kingdom	35.6	52.7	32.6	15.5	4.6	18.8
United States	36.9	55.2	35.2	9.6	10.5	20.4

1. Including undefined for France (1.3), Ireland (0.5), Spain (0.3).
2. Based on end-of-year estimate.
Source: State Planning Organisation, OECD, *Education at a glance,* 1993.

51

Table 18. **Expenditure on education in OECD countries, 1991**

	Public [1]	Effort [2]	Total private and public [1]	Effort [2]
Turkey	**4.0**	**19.9**	–	–
France	5.4	21.1	6.0	23.7
Germany	4.0	–	5.4	28.7
Ireland	5.4	19.5	5.9	21.0
Spain	4.5	19.6	5.6	22.3
Portugal	5.5	27.8	–	–
United Kingdom	5.3	28.1	–	–
United States	5.5	29.6	7.0	29.9
OECD total	5.2	25.9	6.4	27.2

1. As per cent of GDP.
2. Expenditure per student relative to per capita GDP.
Source: OECD, *Education at a glance*, 1993.

(Table 18). Relatively low funding explains persisting shortages of qualified teachers and infrastructure and the failure to meet secondary school target enrolment rates set in the Sixth Five Year Plan.[74] Shortfalls in secondary level vocational training are large, due in part to higher cost per student. By contrast, higher education has expanded quite rapidly over the past decade, reaching 21.5 per cent in 1994 and exceeding the Five Year Plan's target. However, drop out rates are high, due to poor streaming.

Health

In 1993, 60 per cent of the total population was covered by health insurance programmes.[75] In 1991, the share of total expenditure on health as a proportion of total domestic expenditure was 5.16 per cent, compared with an OECD average of 7.8 per cent.[76] In terms of real income per capita (PPP-based), Turkey's health expenditure is at a level commensurate with its income level.

The range of free public health services has been limited and access to service difficult in the Eastern and South-Eastern regions. But, two major health initiatives and the establishment of hospital facilities have recently been targeted to these regions. Infant mortality is a significant problem. It was 49.3 per 1000 live births in 1993 (roughly five to ten times the OECD average). The mortality rate for children under age 5 is 60.9 per 1000 – 50.5 in urban areas and

76.4 in rural areas. This rate represented 17 per cent of total deaths which occur in a year.

Improving income distribution

Data on income distribution are scarce and unreliable, especially in countries with large agricultural populations. In Turkey, available data are fragmentary, but income distribution is widely regarded as relatively unfavourable, with marked disparities between regions.[77] Rough estimates made by the OECD based on latest household income data (see Diagram 14) indicate that income distribution is similar to that in Mexico, but much less equal than in Korea.[78] These comparisons are consistent with differences in basic education levels between these countries. They also suggest that the disparities in per capita GDP and life expectancy between provinces are related to education levels, but this is not conclusive.

Infrastructure can also have a direct bearing on income distribution. The mega-South-Eastern Anatolia Project (GAP) is for example expected to make a

Diagram 14. **INCOME DISTRIBUTION BY DECILE**

As a percentage of total monthly income, 1987

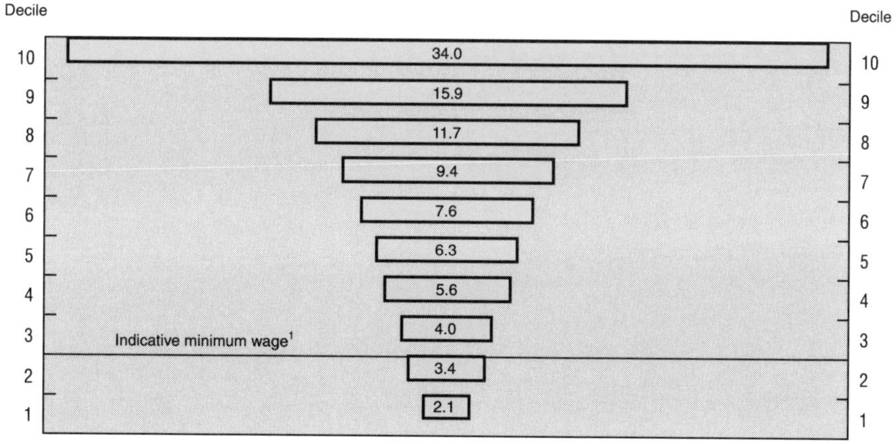

Decile   Decile

Decile	Value
10	34.0
9	15.9
8	11.7
7	9.4
6	7.6
5	6.3
4	5.6
3	4.0
2	3.4
1	2.1

Indicative minimum wage[1]

1. Twice legal minimum wage.
Source: OECD estimates based on *Household Income and Consumption Expenditures Survey*, 1987.

53

major contribution to raising per capita incomes and narrowing regional income differentials in the coming decade. Infrastructure is generally regarded as adequate, but costly and inefficient.[79] There are major shortages in water and sewage facilities due to rapid urbanisation and inadequate urban planning and zoning, which are badly affecting the quality of the environment.[80]

In summary, Turkey's relatively low HDI reading reflects poor health and education outcomes, but a good economic growth record. Subsidies received and deficits run by the SEEs exceeded spending on either health or education in 1993. Education is under-funded, with shortages in qualified teachers, modern teaching methods, teaching materials and supports. These shortages are compounded by low pay for teachers, and the slow adaptation of curricula to the needs of a modern society. Resources could also be allocated more effectively by raising the share going to secondary as opposed to higher education.[81] The health care system is also under-funded. Life expectancy lags behind not only countries with higher income, but also countries with lower incomes (*e.g.* China, Cuba). The latter observation suggests that more effective delivery of health care and female literacy may be as important in determining health outcomes as resources spent. In short, inadequate funding and unequal access to health and education facilities appear to be key in explaining the comparatively low Turkish HDI, as well as the marked urban/rural and geographic disparities within the country.

IV. Conclusions

The Turkish economy has enjoyed comparatively high rates of GDP growth over the past dozen years, aided by the adoption of outward-looking, market-oriented structural policies since the beginning of the 1980s. But macroeconomic imbalances became acute in the late 1980s, as large budget deficits became chronic, inflation averaged 50 to 70 per cent, and international competitiveness deteriorated. Failure to address these imbalances has been costly, as lax fiscal policy and associated money creation has undermined confidence in the currency and the credibility of economic policy. A crisis became inevitable, as the public-sector borrowing requirement (PSBR) soared, despite an overheated economy, to over 12 per cent of GDP in 1993, almost double the budget target, and the current-account deficit widened sharply. January 1994 saw a run on the Turkish lira, triggered by a downgrading of Turkey's sovereign credit rating by two international rating agencies, exacerbating the Treasury's need to draw on Central Bank advances to finance the PSBR. In the event, the Turkish lira plunged by over 70 per cent against the dollar from end-1993 to end-March, despite official intervention. This raised fears of spiralling inflation and instability in the banking system, which were subsequently aggravated by the placing of three small banks under receivership. A radical change in the course of economic policy was clearly required.

The government announced several measures to restore financial market stability. Government guarantees were extended to 100 per cent of individuals' bank deposits. Central Bank control over the financial system was extended, and TL deposits were made more attractive. These regulatory changes, reinforced by the April 1994 stabilisation programme, succeeded in calming financial markets – and the lira, which had fallen to TL 40 000 per US$ in early April, recovered to 31 900 TL/US$ by end-April.

The main feature of the April 1994 programme (which formed the basis for a 14-month stand-by arrangement with the International Monetary Fund concluded in July) was a halving of the PSBR, to TL 243 trillion or 6.2 per cent of GDP, through measures including immediate increases (70 to 100 per cent) in state-controlled prices, one-off tax measures, and a freezing of nominal government spending in spite of higher depreciation-related inflation. The second leg of the package was to accelerate structural reform. Streamlined privatisation legislation was passed quickly by Parliament (though repealed in August by the constitutional court). Budget constraints on SEEs were tightened, the pursuit of commercial goals given prominence, and downsizing or closure of inefficient operations announced. Measures were announced to improve tax administration and to establish a social safety net, and a study was launched on reform of the bankrupt social security system. Initiatives to cut back tax expenditure, to lower border protection, and to introduce competition legislation were also foreshadowed as a run-up to EU customs union by end-1995. In summary, the stabilisation programme's strategy was classic. Macroeconomic policy was to be oriented towards reducing domestic absorption and to locking in a large "real" currency depreciation, while structural reform would boost potential output growth and fiscal consolidation in the medium term.

The first six months of the stabilisation programme saw notable success in cutting the fiscal deficit and in improving the external position. In the event, the 1994 PSBR outcome is estimated at some TL 295 trillion or 7.4 per cent of GDP, slightly more than one-half of the 1993 outcome, despite a more severe drop in output than expected. The small overshooting of the deficit was accounted for by delays in privatisation and higher debt service. There was also a quick improvement in the balance of payments, and exchange market stability was restored. The current account began to improve in the second quarter and registered a surplus of US$2.4 billion for the first nine months of 1994. Foreign debt service was fully met. Imports dropped sharply, and export performance was dynamic. Indeed, the private sector has demonstrated impressive flexibility in adjusting to shocks, raising business optimism concerning the forthcoming EU customs union.

Rapid external adjustment was accompanied by a slowing of short-term net capital outflows, and the TL appreciated modestly in real terms from April to July. The resumption of Treasury borrowing on domestic markets at end-May, albeit at phenomenal interest rates (50 per cent over three months), permitted the debt financing of the PSBR and repayment of some Central Bank advances. Following a drop in August, the real exchange rate stabilised and by mid-November was down some 30 per cent from its level twelve months earlier. Foreign reserves (excluding gold) were rebuilt to pre-crisis levels by July, reaching a record US$7.3 billion by early December. Turkey was removed from credit watch by international credit-rating agencies in late summer, but its rating has yet to be raised.

The big cut in the PSBR, a drop in real wages, and a virtual halt to private-sector borrowing have severely affected output and employment. Real GDP dropped by 11 per cent in the second quarter from its year-earlier level, and there has been a wave of redundancies. OECD estimates are that output fell by almost 5 per cent between 1993 and 1994, twice as much as foreseen in the April plan, partly on account of lower agricultural output. But there are signs that output stopped falling in the third quarter, as industrial capacity utilisation rose, led by strong exports. Business profits are down from their buoyant 1993 levels, but the sharp cut in business investment appears to have left financial balances close to equilibrium, thereby limiting the demand for bank credit.

A crucial shortcoming has been on inflation (the April programme target was for a cumulative 20 per cent price rise in the second half of 1994). The immediate impact of the depreciation and the April hike in public sector tariffs was a 33 per cent jump in the wholesale price index (WPI) between March and April. The monthly rise in the WPI slowed sharply in June and July as these factors waned, but rose to an alarming average monthly rate of 6.7 per cent from September to December, leaving 12-month inflation well into triple digits. With the benefit of hindsight, the stance of monetary policy during the summer proved too easy. With WPI inflation dropping to below 2 per cent a month and optimism rising, interest rates dropped rapidly, reaching 22 per cent a quarter by end-August. But capital inflows were not sufficiently sterilised and broad money grew rapidly. In the event, the resurgence of inflation in the autumn stopped the drop in interest rates, and yields on Treasury bills have risen since mid-October. The official inflation forecast for end-1995 has been revised up to just below 40 per cent in view of stronger underlying inflation in late 1994. But reserve and liquidity requirements were tightened in early 1995.

The immediate policy priority is to rein in inflation, as it is the central element in ensuring coherence of the 1995 budget and, hence, the attainment of a sustainable fiscal position over the medium term. Interest rates may well have to rise substantially in the short term, to contain the excessive growth of money and to underpin a smaller rate of depreciation of the Turkish lira. To illustrate such a process, if nominal depreciation was reduced from the 3 to 4 per cent a month prevailing between August and December to, say, 1 per cent a month, WPI inflation would be reduced by $\frac{1}{2}$ percentage point a month. This, together with higher interest rates, should permit reining in money supply growth to around 1 per cent a month, consistent with lowering 12-month inflation to the revised forecast of some 40 per cent by end-1995. Moreover, a further limited real appreciation of the Turkish lira is unlikely to lead to excessive current-account deficits. The real rate as measured by relative consumer prices has depreciated by some 30 per cent since late 1993, and if this were locked in, the current account as projected by the OECD Secretariat would remain in surplus of around 2 per cent of GDP even when the economy returns to trend output. As Turkey should normally be a net importer of capital in the medium term, there is thus scope to ''trade-off'' some real appreciation for more rapid disinflation.

So long as the 1995 budget targets are adhered to and risk premia on TL debt decline to more normal levels, stabilisation of the debt-to-GDP ratio at sustainable levels is within reach. The 1995 budget presented to Parliament in October targeted a consolidated budget deficit of 3.3 per cent and a total PSBR of 5.1 per cent of GDP. A small increase in the consolidated primary surplus is programmed, but higher debt service may result in only a modest reduction in the PSBR-to-GDP ratio from its 1994-level. With a moderate recovery in output projected in 1995, the output gap will have widened sharply since 1993. Achievement of the 1995 budget targets would thus represent a substantial cut (of around 60 per cent) in the structural deficit in two years. Although tax revenue will be reduced by the loss of ''one-time'' taxes in 1994 and a weaker tax base, these are projected to be offset by improvements in tax administration and by cuts in tax expenditure. The government introduced additional tax measures in January 1995 as a part of a package to increase revenue. On the other hand, while wage restrictions on public sector workers and stringent controls on SEEs' borrowing have been announced, these spending limits may be hard to hold unless inflation comes down in line with official forecasts. Maintaining wage restraint in the public (and private) sectors is key – and would be favoured by lower inflation stemming from "real" currency appreciation.

In the near term, higher interest rates will put temporary pressure on the PSBR. But a temporary rise in the PSBR would be a price well worth paying for reining in inflation, as the immediate risk of a debt explosion is small and would be further attenuated by real currency appreciation. At this juncture, the relevant criterion for fiscal consolidation is the attainment of the targeted total primary budget surplus of some 1 per cent of GDP. Once lower inflation and fiscal consolidation are on track, risk premia on government debt should be progressively, but durably reduced. And this process will be enhanced as Turkey's improved external position facilitates a gradual re-entry into international capital markets and eases domestic crowding-out.

The OECD Secretariat expects the economy to recover gradually, with GDP expanding by 2.8 and 4.5 per cent, respectively, in 1995 and 1996, led by strong exports in response to the large real depreciation. These projections are lower than those in the 1995 budget, on account of an assumed tightening of monetary policy to control higher-than-expected inflation. Given potential output growth of almost 5 per cent, the output gap will widen further in 1995, and this will help to damp inflation, as will lower tariff barriers stemming from EU customs union. A sustained strong competitive position is expected to keep the current account in surplus in 1995-96. Inflation is projected to fall sharply from 120 per cent on average in 1994 to around 70 per cent in 1995 and 40 per cent in 1996. These projections allow for higher end-1994 inflation, but assume that policy will act to hold inflation through 1995 in line with the revised targets. They are heavily dependent on achieving the targeted total primary budget surplus, and an eventual fall in the risk premia embodied in nominal interest rates.

Experience in other OECD countries is that building confidence and lowering risk premia take time, and would be greatly enhanced if policy was framed in a coherent medium-term context with clear policy rules. A first step would be to adopt explicit targets for debt and deficit to GDP ratios. The OECD Secretariat's medium-term scenario suggests that, assuming that the 1995 budget targets are met, the PSBR would be 5 close to 4 per cent of GDP by the year 2000. Given high potential growth in Turkey, this would be consistent with a stable debt-to-GDP ratio of around 40 per cent, though it would be prudent to aim at smaller structural deficits. A second element is to set clear priorities among spending programmes as the total budget envelope shrinks. Resources in public sector activities are clearly not being used optimally. Interest on the public debt exceeds expenditure on either health or education, and standards in these areas (particularly in the rural and eastern parts of the country) lag well behind some countries with comparable per capita incomes. One of the few robust empirical relations in cross-country comparisons of economic growth is the high dividends to basic education and their spin-offs for better health outcomes and higher productivity levels. A third critical requirement is to build in mechanisms which help to attain fiscal targets: US pay-as-you-go budget provisions or sequestration – mandatory cuts in lower-priority spending in the case of failure to attain targeted deficits – are examples. In the Turkish context, this would require as a minimum that supplementary budgets were restricted to such unforeseen events as natural disasters.

Last, but not least, it is critical to set up an anti-inflationary monetary policy, and to build a constituency for low inflation. The re-orientation of monetary policy for 1995 discussed above could be a first step towards establishing a nominal anchor in the medium term within a clear anti-inflationary policy framework. The new Central Bank law which sets out a steady reduction in Treasury's access to Central Bank financing is to be welcomed. But a minimum recourse to such facilities would enhance monetary control. To be sure, the Turkish economy has performed reasonably well in terms of growth over the past dozen years. But experience in the High-Performing Asian and Latin-American economies suggests that economic performance could have been far better with low inflation. High inflation has gradually but surely sapped the strength of the economy through, *inter alia*, the shortening of planning horizons of business and government, poor quality of investment, and the diversion of scarce resources towards "living with inflation" rather than creating wealth. Finally, high inflation has eroded Turkish citizens' trust in their own currency and in its institutions. In short, a substantial improvement in macroeconomic balances is within reach. But a medium-term policy framework with strong policy rules and a nominal anchor are needed to consolidate the gains made immediately after the introduction of the April programme.

Medium-term economic prospects for the Turkish economy are fundamentally bright, due to a rich endowment of physical and human resources. The private sector has demonstrated impressive dynamism and flexibility in adapting to shocks. However, more rapid and vigorous progress in structural reform is needed not only to facilitate continuing fiscal consolidation but also to further enhance the efficiency of the economy generally. Following a long hiatus, prospects for more rapid progress in structural reform have improved – the financial crisis and imminent EU customs union obliging the government to face the consequences of a bloated, inefficient public sector.

Notwithstanding delays in the "high-profile" privatisation programme, encouraging signs are emerging of progress in rationalising the public sector. Agricultural subsidies were cut in 1994, and are being held at lower levels in the 1995 budget. Tax administration is being improved through better auditing, computerisation and higher tax penalties, and the tax base is being widened by reducing the plethora of tax exemptions. State economic enterprises (SEEs) are being downsized and made more efficient, and some large loss-making SEEs are scheduled to be closed. The lifting of the ban on the sequestration of SEEs' and municipalities' assets (in the event of commercial or tax arrears) is obliging State managers to operate with clearer commercial goals. Revised privatisation legislation has been approved by Parliament and should lead to medium-term improvements in economic efficiency. Future privatisation revenue will be kept off-budget, and will be used for retraining, redundancy pay, restructuring SEEs to raise efficiency, and retiring SEEs' debt. These are positive steps, but further investment channelled to the SEEs needs to be subject to clear commercial criteria and ceilings. Draft legislation is being prepared to modify social security contribution rates and retirement ages, although much more rapid and radical reform will be necessary to achieve financial solvency. Much also remains to be done to streamline tariffs, *ad hoc* foreign trade taxes, subsidies and tax exemptions. Such reform would help to shift the incentive structure away from economic rent seeking towards wealth creation.

In conclusion, OECD *Economic Surveys* have argued for some years now that reduction of the public borrowing requirement was central to the restoration of Turkey's economic health. The authorities have announced a succession of deficit-reduction plans over the years, but these have not been met. This was partly due to insufficient political commitment to budgetary retrenchment, perhaps understandable at a time when economic performance continued to be rather favourable in a number of respects in spite of high inflation and public borrowing. But more fundamentally, the deficit-reduction plans were probably unrealistic in the absence of thorough-going reforms of some of the structural features of the public sector, and notably the SEEs. The 1994 crisis made strong action imperative, both immediately and on a more sustained basis. The increasing sensitivity of international capital markets to sovereign risks heightens the need for such action.

The authorities have achieved considerable short-term success in stabilising financial-market conditions through a series of one-off tax and spending measures. But lasting stability is not assured. Much of the improvement in macroeconomic balances reflects the effects of drops in real incomes, a "real" depreciation and depressed domestic demand. Lasting economic expansion led by exports and private investment will depend on reining in inflation, fundamental structural reform and sustained medium-term fiscal consolidation. Significant delays in structural reform and fiscal consolidation risk further financial market instability and permanently higher risk premia, thereby jeopardising economic growth. Conversely, meeting the 1995 budget targets and accelerating structural reform could relatively soon result in a virtuous circle and support the realisation of Turkey's undoubtedly bright medium-term economic potential.

Notes

1. This year's survey uses the "new" GDP series for the first time. The "old" series was based on 1968 production weights and partial information. The "new" series incorporate data from the Agricultural Product Marketing Survey, the Annual Survey of Manufacturing Industry, the Household Labour Survey, the 1987 Household Income and Expenditure Survey, and special studies of the construction, transport and trade industries. The new estimates raised the level of GDP by some 30 per cent compared with previous estimates, and correspondingly lowered a number of key ratios customarily expressed as percentages of GDP.

2. Capacity utilisation rose from 66.4 per cent to 73 per cent between the second and third quarters of 1994.

3. Despite significant improvements in the quality of the "new" GDP series, the size of the informal economy is unknown. Some estimates place it at some one-third of total economic activity. To some extent, the lack of a data base reflects the large proportion of self-employed. Agriculture represented 42.8 per cent of the labour force in 1993 and there are numerous small businesses for which data are limited. Dependent employment represents only a quarter of total employment. These features explain the lack of fully articulated household- and business-sector income and expenditure accounts, but also the flexibility of the private sector and its capacity to adjust to shocks.

4. M2Y consists of M2 plus domestic foreign-exchange deposits, and is thus a very broad measure of money supply.

5. The lag between changes in the exchange-rate and import prices are estimated to be very short, with most imports priced in foreign currencies. As imports are around 20 per cent of GDP, the appreciation in the price of foreign currency of 62 per cent between March and April would have mechanically raised the price level by 12 per cent in a month.

6. The forecast for the second half of 1994 was to reduce monthly rates of inflation to less than 3 per cent on average, so as to permit targeting an annual rate of inflation of some 20 per cent during 1995.

7. By contrast, public-sector prices rose by only 3.1 per cent a month until November, but increased by 12 per cent in December as a result of some large adjustments in a number of State economic enterprises.

8. Real labour costs of workers in the public service fell by an estimated 8 per cent; civil servants' salaries dropped some 26 per cent and the real minimum wage by 21 per cent in 1994.

9.   Short-term capital liabilities increased by US$6.3 billion and long-term borrowing by US$4.9 billion.

10. Of which US$4.3 billion in interest payments and US$5.2 billion in repayment of principal. A current-account surplus of some US$3 billion was recorded in 1994. Foreign capital inflows were around US$4 billion. This and a slowdown in short-term capital outflows permitted servicing of the foreign debt as well as substantial reserve accumulation.

11. The higher foreign debt burden largely reflected a drop in GDP measured in US dollars. Total external debt was estimated at US$67.3 billion at end-1993. Notwithstanding the payment of US$5.2 billion in capital payments in 1994, end-1994 foreign debt is estimated at some US$64.7 billion. This high figure also reflected *inter alia* the effective depreciation of the dollar of some 10 per cent and the 53.7 per cent share of foreign debt in non-US currencies. Some two-thirds of foreign debt is at fixed interest rates and its average maturity is around 12.5 years.

12. Industry has typically relied on retained profits to finance investment. Hence, investment may not prove to be too sensitive to high interest rates.

13. Total public sector borrowing exceeded programme targets by TL 123 trillion, with higher interest payments accounting for TL 43 trillion and higher consolidated budget spending on personnel contributing TL 24 trillion to the over-run.

14. Central Bank money growth in the twelve months to December accelerated from 43 per cent in 1990 to 65 per cent in 1993.

15. This is based on the OECD Secretariat measure of trade-weighted exchange rate, with the price of foreign exchange defined as the value of a Turkish lira per unit of foreign currency.

16. Commercial banks' open foreign-currency positions were reported to be US$4.9 billion at end-1993.

17. Prior to the run on the Turkish lira, commercial banks found it profitable to borrow abroad and lend domestically at "high" rates. Such operations would not normally be profitable, as an expected depreciation of the TL would essentially offset the interest rate differentials. But foreign borrowing, having had a bandwagon effect, held up the "real" exchange rate at artificially high levels. This continued until the exchange market collapse. The banks that eventually closed were TYT Bank, Marbank, and Impeksbank. Between them, they accounted for less than 1 per cent of total bank deposits.

18. Depositors have no incentive to monitor bank solvency, and this guarantee removes the incentive for banks to steer clear of high-risk strategies when competing for deposits.

19. An incomplete list includes Israel, Argentina, Brazil, Bolivia, Mexico, Chile, Poland and Turkey. For a review of recent stabilisation experience see Bruno *et al.* (1991), *"Lessons of Economic Stabilization and its Aftermath"*, MIT Press, London, and OECD, *1991/92 Economic Survey of Mexico*, Paris.

20. These included a 10 per cent surcharge on personal and corporate incomes, a net asset tax on businesses including banks and increases on real estate and motor vehicle taxes.

21. Delays to the privatisation programme meant that Turkey was unable to draw on a planned structural adjustment loan from the World Bank.

22. Around one-fifth of this rise reflected the effects of the TL appreciation *vis-à-vis* the dollar of some 8 per cent over this period.

23. Such calculations unfortunately give no time path for achieving steady-state solutions. These are iterated in an illustrative medium-term baseline scenario (see Annex III).

24. Civil servants, however, receive more generous pensions benefits.

25. This formula does not, however, ensure Central Bank control over advances to the Treasury. For example, the TL 100 trillion October 1994 supplementary budget automatically increased the Treasury's borrowing line by TL 15 trillion, even though it was not used.

26. Simple interest rates on 3-month Treasury bills fell from 50 per cent a quarter at the beginning of June to 21 per cent a quarter at the beginning of October. These interest rates would imply real interest rates of between 40 to 50 per cent a year based on official inflation forecasts of a 20 per cent actual rise in the price level in the second half of 1994. But *ex post*, inflation in late 1994 was roughly 50 per cent higher than this target and, hence, real *ex ante* interest rates correspondingly lower.

27. OECD Secretariat analysis indicates that the current real exchange rate if held would yield a current-account surplus of roughly 1 1/2 to 2 per cent of GDP. A real appreciation of the TL of some 20 per cent would be consistent with a zero current-account deficit (see Annex III).

28. High economic growth in the HPAEs was reinforced by the priority attached to raising basic education levels. Educational attainment rates for secondary-plus levels of schooling were around 70 per cent in Hong Kong, Singapore, Taiwan and South Korea in 1990. In Turkey, only 13.7 per cent of males had completed high-school education or higher in 1990, while the ratio for females was 7.8 per cent (see Chapter III).

29. Use of the exchange rate as a nominal anchor was part of the Mexican stabilisation strategy. The December 1994 exchange market crisis suggests that a rigid anchor may well help to lower inflation, but may also lead to an over-valued exchange rate and, ultimately, to a collapse of the policy.

30. In 1992, there were 42 SEEs including those transferred to the privatisation agency (PPA). Data published in September 1994 indicate that the State sector employed 2.76 million people, of which 650 000 were in SEEs or 3.6 per cent of total employment.

31. Provisional estimates for 1994 indicate that SEEs deficits were reduced to 2.6 per cent of GDP, while transfers dropped to 0.65 per cent of GDP. The figures cited are based on the new GDP series; the old series would raise these ratios by roughly one-third.

32. Debt/equity ratios (including balance sheet profits) were 236.6 per cent in 1993 for public firms compared with 140.4 per cent for private firms (for sources see Table 11).

33. Australian experience appears quite typical of the large efficiency gains possible through introducing rational incentive structures in SEEs. For details see OECD, *1993/94 Economic Survey of Australia*, Paris.

34. Estimates of TFP growth for large private sector firms of 3.9 per cent from 1983 to 1992 are relatively high compared with other OECD countries. The fact that all large firm TFP was only 0.5 per cent indicates the influence of SEEs. Data for 1993 indicate a cyclical pick-up in TFP in both the private (14.9 per cent) and public (12.1 per cent) sectors, but the gap between the sectors gave no sign of narrowing. Official TFP estimates for the total economy are not

available. OECD estimates suggest whole economy TFP growth of 2.5 per cent in 1983-92 (Annex IV).

35. In 1992, the shares of wages and salaries in sales income were 9.47 per cent in the private sector and 18.97 per cent in public sector firms. The shares of financial expenditure in sales income were 4.79 and 10.37 per cent respectively. For details see O. Ertuna (1993), ''The Position of Public Enterprises Among the Major 500 Industrial Concerns'', *Journal of the Istanbul Chamber of Commerce*, September, pp. 100-104. These data suggest that public-sector firms could produce the same output with one-half of the labour and one-third of the capital inputs presently used. In 1993 public-sector firms recorded sharp increases in output and TFP, although investment funds have been sharply restricted over the past several years.

36. These include the TDCI (Iron and Steel Company), TTK (Coal Company), TEK (Electricity Company), TSFAS (Sugar Company), TMO (Soil Products Office), TEKEL (Tobacco and Alcoholic Beverages Company) and TCDD (State Railways). The financing limits set for cumulative changes since 31 December 1993 are TL 2.3 trillion for 31 March 1994, and TL 55 trillion 31 December 1994. Preliminary indications are that these limits will be attained (see Chapter II).

37. TTK (coal) has laid off almost 5 000 workers and 3 500 more workers will be laid off by year-end. The plan is to close down loss-making coal mines and to further reduce employment levels by 5 000 to 21 307. Studies for restructuring, privatisation or closure of TÜPRAS (oil refinery) and Sümerbank have been accelerated.

38. To date one (mine) of the announced closures has taken place. By the end of 1994, seven enterprises are scheduled to be closed including: Sümer Holding (Textile), the Yarmica facilities of Petkim, Petlas A.S. (Tire company), five city hotels managed by TURBAN, the Aydin enterprises of TESTAS (Turkish Electronical Measurement Equipment Company), the Halic Camialti and Alaybey dockyards and the combines and enterprises of EBK, DMO (State Material Company), the Ankara Beer Factory owned by TEKEL (Turkish Tobacco Products Monopoly), the Bomonti Beer Factory and the Cibali Cigar Factory. Operation of KARDEMIR (Karabük Iron and Steel company) and TZDK (Turkish Agricultural Equipment Company) were to be stopped at end-1994 if they could not be privatised or taken over by their workers. Preparatory work on the possible closure of KARDEMIR complex was completed, but the government announced in November that the Karabük plant would be rehabilitated over the coming 30 months with the government assuming all past debt. It was then handed over to the workers and local residents for one lira.

39. The World Bank has estimated that about 23 per cent of SEEs, representing 13 per cent of fixed assets and 21 per cent of employment in the sector, are not viable and are candidates for closure. To make such closures socially acceptable, policies of labour redeployment, retraining and the establishment of a social safety net are needed. See *World Bank Report*, No. 11903-TU, 1993, pp. 86-87.

40. For example, it appears that only 50 per cent of water is billed and of this only 60 per cent is collected. A further problem is that the setting of public utility rates is highly politicised. Introduction of private sector management would thus significantly weaken, if not eliminate this constraint.

41. Of this total, some three quarters represented sales of minority stakes in private companies, with the rest representing actual asset sales in peripheral sectors. In 1986, 127 enterprises were included in the privatisation programme. In March 1994, of these enterprises, seven were excluded and 73 enterprises had been privatised. Of the 47 enterprises remaining to be privatised, there are 21 with a State share of less than 50 per cent, and 26 with a State share of more than 50 per cent.

42. Of the total sales revenue obtained *via* privatisation of $2.76 billion, block sales were $0.81 billion; public sales $0.42 billion; international institutional offers $0.32 billion; the Istanbul stockmarket $0.5 billion; and 16 foundations $0.01 billion. Dividend revenue totalled $0.7 billion over this period. See *Public Participation Administration Monthly Report*, September 1994.

43. Around one-third of the original revenue estimates were earmarked for redundancy payments, retraining of displaced workers and the operating expenses of the PPA. The original 1994 programme called for full privatisation of two firms, and partial or full privatisation of eight other firms by the end of 1994. Pre-privatisation studies for the electricity company (TEK) and PTT (post, telephone and telegraph) were to be completed by end-1994 with the goal of privatising them in 1995. Two banks were also to be privatised and another bank open to public participation.

44. Extensive preparations have already taken place, so it should be possible to conclude a number of sales quickly, subject to market conditions. The precise method of sale will be determined on a case-by-case basis. In general, foreign ownership will be permitted, although restrictions may be applied where an industry is thought to have strategic importance. Early candidates for privatisation include Petrol Ofisi (petroleum retailer), Sümerbank, Eregli (iron and steel), Turkish Airlines, Petlas (tire manufacturer), Tüpras (oil refinery) and Havas (airport ground handling).

45. The main differences from the previous bill are that privatisation revenue will not be used for budgetary investments or spending. Revenue is to be used for repayment of outstanding debts, restructuring and/or to raise the efficiency of SEEs. Furthermore, redundancy payments and/or early retirement are to be more generous; anti-cartel measures have been taken to prevent the transfer of monopolies from the public to the private sector; the government will hold a ''golden share'' in strategic industries (including Turkish airlines, TMO Alkaloid and Turkish Petroleum); and insider trading will be formally illegal.

46. See OECD, *1993/94 Economic Survey of Turkey*, Chapter III, Paris.

47. See OECD (1994), *Agricultural Policies, Markets and Trade: Monitoring and Outlook 1994*, pp. 162-64, and *National Policies and Agricultural Trade: Country Study Turkey*, Paris.

48. Comparable figures for consumer subsidy equivalents in 1993 were 33 per cent for Turkey and 34 per cent for the OECD average.

49. This was one consideration for the shift from agricultural price supports to deficiency payments in Mexico in 1994.

50. For example, the 20 per cent fertiliser subsidy will now be collected by farmers (rather than producers) *via* the Agricultural bank.

51. Transfers to SEEs in 1994 were originally programmed at TL 36.5 trillion, versus an estimated outcome of TL 21.5 trillion. In August 1994, the Union of Agricultural Sales

Cooperatives announced support prices for hazelnuts, and an extension of support prices to unlined cotton, sultana grapes and sunflower seed, in line with world prices. Support purchases are being made with the cooperatives' resources and they bear the financial risk. The extension of support prices in the absence of measures to restrict excess supply can be costly. Measures have therefore been taken to reduce tobacco and tea output through acreage restrictions, and the open-ended purchases of some commodities (*e.g.* cotton) without quality controls have been restricted.

52. Individuals who take on a new (private sector) job after early retirement (from the public sector) are not obliged to make further public pension contributions, despite working and drawing pension.

53. In many OECD countries, potential pension rights represent a major medium-term threat for fiscal stabilisation, due to the rapidly rising average age of the population. For Turkey, this problem is more distant, but with very short working life contributions, the system is actuarially insolvent, unless radical changes in entitlement and contribution rates are made. Draft legislation in parliament would be a step forward, but would not establish full actuarial solvency.

54. See OECD, *Revenue Statistics 1965-93*, Paris, 1994.

55. There are seven tax rates including a zero rate. The highest is 55 per cent. The lowest non-zero rate is 25 per cent and begins at the comparatively modest level of TL 150 million (in January 1995). Social security charges can add some 30 to 35 per cent to total non-wage labour costs. Hence, for the average production worker, the tax load in Turkey ranks among the highest in OECD countries (above that in the United States, Japan, Germany, France, Italy, the United Kingdom, Norway, etc.).

56. The general VAT rate was raised from 12 to 15 per cent, for basic foodstuffs from 6 to 8 per cent and for luxury goods from 20 to 23 per cent. The zero rate (mainly applying to exports and some exempted imports) and the 1 per cent rate (mainly applying to agricultural products) remained largely unchanged. The five different VAT rates complicate administration and hinder tax efficiency, but can be defended on the grounds of equity. For details see OECD, *Economic Surveys of Turkey 1993/94* and *1991/92*, Chapter III, Paris.

57. Administrative costs are lower than for income taxes. Evasion is more difficult. The regressive effects of indirect tax are partly offset by lower rates on basic necessities, albeit at the expense of tax efficiency. Finally, expenditure taxes as opposed to income taxes theoretically favour saving by avoiding the double taxation of capital income.

58. The arithmetic average of levies on imports such as the Mass Housing Fund currently average 17 per cent. This tax reduces efficiency by raising border protection. Hence, its phasing out in 1995 should be efficient, albeit at the expense of lost revenue. See GATT, *ibid.*, 1993, p. 48.

59. The government is receiving assistance from the World Bank to improve administration and collection procedures. Initiatives include improvements in tax audits, tighter accounting and tax registration requirements. Computerisation of the tax system is to be completed in 1995, and will permit enforcement through the cross-checking of tax returns. Penalties for fraud and late payment have also been raised, the latter to 12 per cent a month. A draft law includes measures to capture the unrecorded activities, including issuing everyone a tax number. It is

difficult to estimate the effects of better administration, but tax collection might have been boosted by TL 8 trillion in 1994 and might rise a further TL 20 trillion in 1995 due to these improvements.

60. Advance payments (based on previous years' tax assessments) have been raised from 50 to 70 per cent for corporate income and from 30 to 50 per cent for personal income tax. Such changes reduce the "real" revenue losses from higher inflation, but cannot fully offset them given inevitable payment lags. High inflation can also lead to revenue losses, if domestic residents borrow domestically to purchase foreign assets. In the event of depreciation, capital gains on foreign assets are lightly taxed, while the borrower benefits from full deductibilty of nominal interest costs.

61. See "Annual Review of Industrial Policies and Situation in Industry: Contribution of Turkey", OECD Industry Committee, Paris, 1994.

62. Low inflation would reduce these distortions and improve equity as well. It is difficult to judge the post-tax effects of the system on income distribution, as the present "system" faces major problems from under-reporting. Ultimately, relying on the "inflation tax" may be more regressive than widening the tax base and raising VAT rates.

63. For example, a number of one-time taxes were introduced in the April 1994 programme, including: a 10 per cent surcharge on personal and corporate income taxes; a net asset tax on businesses, including banks; supplements to real estate and motor vehicle taxes; and higher stamp taxes, fees and excises on fuel. These were necessary to raise revenue, but one-off taxes (especially if they tax capital) do not improve tax efficiency.

64. Voluntary export restraints apply in the textiles and clothing sector. The textiles industry negotiated an agreement with the EU on textiles in 1982 and on clothing in 1986. Bilateral restraints under the Multi Fibre Arrangement have been negotiated with the USA and Canada. Those with Sweden and Austria have ended.

65. The 1993 import regime consolidated most supplementary import charges into the Mass Housing Fund levy. See GATT, *Trade Policy Review Mechanism: The Republic of Turkey*, 20 December 1993, p. vii and p. 50.

66. A 1990 study based on tariffs, additional surcharges and tax concessions on imported goods estimated that the effective rate of protection had dropped from 19.2 per cent in 1985 to 9.1 per cent in 1989 (based on total imports); see OECD, *1991/92 Economic Survey of Turkey*, p. 81, Paris. A more recent estimate (based on dutiable imports) indicates that effective tariff rates dropped steadily from 78.8 per cent in 1984, 53.8 per cent in 1989 and to 38.4 per cent by 1991 – with a bias towards protecting export industries. See GATT, *ibid.*, 1993, p. 145.

67. See GATT, *ibid.*, p. 65.

68. The three-firm concentration ratio across 50 selected products was 86 per cent in 1988-90.

69. UNDP, *Report on the National Launching of the 1994 UNDP Human Development*, 23 June 1994, Ankara, Turkey.

70. In 1990 Turkey ranked 71st among 173 countries. But the disparity between regions was stark. There were 52 provinces (urban areas) above this average, of which 20 ranked among the high, 29 medium and 3 among UN low development areas. By contrast, no rural areas

(provinces) ranked among the high, 32 were among the medium and 45 among the UN low development regions. In terms of absolute differences, the province of Mugla had a reading of 0.906 on the human development index, while the rural area of Van was 0.221 (slightly above Togo with 0.218 but below Haiti). A number of caveats are attached to these estimates. In particular, the unrecorded economy may be larger in rural as opposed to urban areas, thereby overstating the degree of disparity. See UNDP, Report on the First National Human Development Conference, Ankara, September 1992.

71. This relation is illustrated in the HPAEs: in the 1960s, rapidly rising education levels were reflected in a sharp slowing in population growth to rates similar to the OECD average by the 1980s. The sharp drop in Turkish live birth rates since the 1960s is also consistent with the big rise in female literacy rates over this period.

72. Addressing these backlogs will require resources for basic education, including special programmes for older people and women.

73. Data are not available for private education in Turkey, but given its small role, its inclusion would further lower Turkey's relative effort (*i.e.* expenditure per student relative to per capita GDP).

74. Enrolment rates at the pre-school level in 1992 were 5.0 per cent, compared with the 8.5 per cent target in the Sixth Plan. In primary schools, the 100 per cent target enrolment rate was achieved as compulsory education is currently five years, but the secondary school rate was 60.1 per cent, compared with a target of 73 per cent. But, the upper secondary school enrolment rate of 41.7 per cent exceeded the target. Only 50 per cent of the demand for vocational and technical education was met in urban areas, although there is excess capacity in the schools of small settlements. By contrast, in higher education the enrolment rate of 16.4 per cent in 1992 exceeded the target. See *Sixth Five Year Plan (1990-94)*, State Planning Organisation, 1993, pp. 109-10.

75. Since the law on socialisation of health services (1961), the government has been committed to a programme of rationalisation of public health services with the objective of providing primary health care in rural areas and developing preventive and curative services.

76. See OECD Health Data Base.

77. *Ibid.*, State Planning Organisation, p. 110.

78. See OECD, *1993/94 Economic Survey of Korea*, p. 27, and *1991/92 Economic Survey of Mexico*, p. 22.

79. The transport and communications systems (important features in attracting foreign investment) are good, albeit costly and inefficient (*e.g.* the railroads have a large number of inefficient short haul lines, leading to substantial losses).

80. Increased private-sector participation in public infrastructure is also expected (*e.g.* electricity generation, dams, irrigation and roads in South-East Anatolia) following the passage of Build-Operate-Transfer (BOT) legislation. BOT will allow the private sector to build and operate "public" utilities on a stable long-term basis, before ultimately transferring the assets to the public sector. BOT may help to mobilise private capital for public infrastructure and perhaps raise overall investment.

81. In the HPAEs, there is strong evidence that rates of return on human capital are highest for primary and secondary schooling, dropping off sharply with higher education. These are among the few robust empirical results found in studies explaining cross-country differences in economic growth. See World Bank, *The East Asian Miracle*, 1993.

Annex I

Determinants of wholesale price inflation in Turkey

The wholesale price index (WPI) is a good measure of inflation pressures in Turkey. The monthly change in the WPI inflation is reasonably well explained by growth of the money supply (M2), and depreciation of the Turkish lira/dollar exchange rate. The regression equation was estimated for the period July 1986 to May 1994, and included dummy variables to account for the tendency for wholesale price inflation to rise in January and fall in June of each year and a dummy variable to account for the exceptional increase in wholesale prices in April 1994 (Table A1).[1]

The estimated relation has the following features:

i) In the long run, the level of the WPI is determined by the money supply. WPI inflation adjusts to M2 growth with a lag of four to eight months: a 1 percentage point increase in M2 leads to a 0.32 percentage point increase in WPI inflation after four months, rising to 0.45 percentage points after eight months, 0.52 percentage points after a year, and 1 percentage point in the long run.

ii) Changes in the exchange rate have an immediate impact on WPI inflation. The impact of the exchange rate (0.20) is close to the share of imports in GDP.

iii) The coefficient on past wholesale price inflation implies relatively low inertia in monthly inflation, with temporary shocks to the price level having little impact on wholesale price inflation after two months.

The equation predicts actual inflation outturns well in the out-of-sample period. In particular the low monthly figures last June and July, and the subsequent pick-up from August to November are well tracked (Table A2). The inflation outturn for December was not so well predicted, but this partly reflects the bringing-forward of State economic enterprise price increases that have typically occurred in January. The recent acceleration in WPI is explained by rapid growth of M2 in the second and third quarters (average monthly increases of 18 per cent between March and June, and 6 per cent between June and September).

This relation suggests that the target to bring 12-month inflation down to around 40 per cent by December 1995 would require restricting the growth of M2 to 1 per cent a month and holding nominal exchange-rate depreciation to 1 per cent a month. Attaining these conditions could bring monthly WPI inflation below 4 per cent in February 1995 and down to 2½ per cent in May.

Table A1. **Regression for wholesale prices** [1]

Explanatory variable	Coefficient	T-ratio
Constant	−0.23675	1.0
Growth of wholesale prices (−1)	0.26149	4.4
Growth of exchange rate (TL/US$)	0.19639	3.0
Growth of M2	0.09969	1.9
Growth of M2 (−1)	−0.08115	1.2
Growth of M2 (−2)	−0.02982	0.5
Growth of M2 (−3)	0.08091	1.4
Growth of M2 (−4)	0.12769	2.3
Log (wholesale prices/M2) (−1)	−0.02292	1.1
Dummy for April 1994	0.13116	3.9
Dummy for January	0.02748	3.7
Dummy for June	−0.02874	4.4
Regression standard error	0.0162	
Diagnostic statistics: [2]		
Serial correlation	$F_{(12,71)} = 0.75$	
Functional form	$F_{(1,82)} = 0.00$	
Normality	Chi-Square $(2) = 30.26$	
Heteroscedasticity	$F_{(1,93)} = 0.11$	

Note: Growth of a variable is defined as the change in its logarithm.
1. Dependent variable: monthly growth of wholesale prices. Period: July 1986 to May 1994, monthly data.
2. The tests indicate that the regression error-terms are not normally distributed, but that the regression is otherwise well-specified.
Source: OECD.

Table A2. **Regression predictions of monthly wholesale price inflation**

	Prediction	Outturn	Error
1994 June [1]	−0.9	1.9	−2.8
July	2.1	0.9	1.2
August	3.8	2.7	1.1
September	7.3	5.4	1.9
October	6.7	6.9	−0.2
November	6.5	6.4	0.1
December	4.1	8.3	−4.2
1995 January [2, 3]	7.2	8.4	−1.2
February	3.6	..	..
March	3.6	..	..
April	3.6	..	..
May	2.4	..	..
June [1]	−0.9	..	..

1. Predictions for June include a decline of 2.9 per cent from the seasonal dummy variable.
2. Predicted values for January onwards assume growth of M2 of 1 per cent a month from January 1995, and depreciation of the exchange rate is 1 per cent a month from February 1995.
3. Prediction for January includes an increase of 2.7 per cent from the seasonal dummy variable.
Source: OECD.

Note

1. An alternative version of this regression tested for the inclusion of a measure of the "output gap", but found it to be insignificant. Similar regressions were estimated (but are not reported here) for M1 and M2Y. These relations give quite similar results for the key parameters, *i.e.* exchange-rate changes and lagged money.

Annex II

The financeable public sector deficit in the medium term

This annex presents an analysis of the financeable public-sector deficit.

The financeable deficit is defined as the level of the budget deficit (or surplus) that is consistent with a constant ratio of government debt to GDP, and a constant rate of inflation.[1] The financeable deficit is given by the following equation:

$$d/y = (g - r) b/y + (p + g) m/y + (g - r^* - e - er^*) b^*/y$$

where:

d/y = primary deficit as a proportion of GDP,
g = growth rate of real GDP,
r = real rate of interest on debt denominated in domestic currency,
r^* = real rate of interest on debt denominated in foreign currency,
b/y = government debt denominated in domestic currency as a proportion of GDP,
b^*/y = government debt denominated in foreign currency as a proportion of GDP,
p = rate of inflation,
m/y = ratio of reserve money to GDP,
e = rate of depreciation of real exchange rate.

Table A3 shows two cases, indicative of the conditions prevailing in Turkey. In the short term, the real interest rate on Treasury debt is above its medium-term level, while projected growth is below its medium-term trend. Both factors increase the financeable surplus, but high inflation partially offsets this. Nevertheless, in order to keep the debt-to-GDP ratio below 50 per cent in the face of high real interest rates, it will be necessary to aim at a primary public-sector surplus of around 2 per cent in the short term.

As stabilisation policies acquire credibility, the risk premium embodied in high real interest rates on Treasury debt should decline, enabling stabilisation to be maintained with a lower primary surplus. The table indicates that medium-term GDP growth of 5 per cent, combined with real interest rates of around 10 per cent on Turkish lira-denominated debt, inflation of 10 per cent per annum and a debt-to-GDP ratio of 50 per cent could be achieved with a primary public-sector surplus of around 1 per cent of GDP.

The table also presents a number of variants on the medium-term scenario. In the base case, it is assumed that the real interest rate on debt denominated in Turkish lira falls to 10 per cent per annum in the medium term. As macroeconomic policy gains credibility, lower risk premia could be demanded on Turkish assets. If the real rate fell to 8 per cent per annum (variant 1), a primary surplus of only 1/4 per cent per annum would be necessary to obtain the base case scenario's inflation and debt to GDP outcomes.

Table A3. **Medium-term financeable fiscal balances**

Financeable primary balance, per cent of GDP[1]

Short-term stabilisation [2,3]	1.8
Medium-term stabilisation [2,4]	0.7
Variants on medium-term stabilisation	
1. Real interest rate to 8 per cent	0.2
2. Debt/GDP ratio to 35 per cent	1.2
3. Real GDP growth 7 per cent	−0.4
4. Inflation target 5 per cent	1.0

1. Positive numbers indicate a primary surplus.
2. The medium-term and short-term stabilisations both assume:
    Trend real interest rate on foreign currency debt 6 per cent (r* = 0.06).
    Targeted ratio of lira-dominated debt to GDP 25 per cent (b/y = 0.25).
    Targeted ratio of foreign currency debt to GDP 25 per cent (b*/y = 0.25).
    Ratio of reserve money to GDP 5 per cent (m/y = 0.05).
3. The short-term stabilisation assumes:
    Rate of real GDP growth 4 per cent per annum (g = 0.04).
    Real interest rate on lira-denominated debt 20 per cent (r = 0.20).
    Targeted rate of inflation 50 per cent (p = 0.5).
4. The medium-term stabilisation assumes:
    Rate of real GDP growth 5 per cent per annum (g = 0.05).
    Real interest rate on lira-denominated debt 10 per cent (r = 0.10).
    Targeted rate of inflation 10 per cent (p = 0.1).
Source: OECD.

In the short run, a larger deficit than the financeable balance can be financed by a build-up of debt. However, in the medium term, the financeable surplus necessary is higher (variant 2), as debt service is larger. Indeed, it is likely that the financeable surplus would be greater than shown in variant 2, as higher debt to GDP ratios would drive up risk premia and real interest rates.

In the event of substantial reform of State economic enterprises (SEEs), privatisation and reform of the tax and social security systems, the trend rate of growth could approach that achieved by the High-Performing Asian Economies (HPAEs). If the trend rate of growth were to rise from 5 to say 7 per cent per annum, it would be feasible to run a small primary deficit (variant 3).

Finally, the base case targets an inflation rate of 10 per cent per annum. A more ambitious inflation target of 5 per cent per annum would imply a financeable surplus of 1 per cent of GDP (variant 4).

Note

1. The analysis is derived from Anand and Wijnbergen (1989), ''Inflation and the financing of government expenditure: an introductory analysis with an application to Turkey'', *World Bank Economic Review,* Vol. 3, No. 1. It assumes that each of the key variables are at medium-term trend levels, and does not seek to explain the effects of short-term deviations from these trends. See also Özatay, F. (1992), ''Sustainability of fiscal deficits, monetary policy and inflation stabilisation'', *The Case of Turkey,* Discussion Paper No. 9209, Central Bank of Turkey.

Annex III

Medium-term fiscal stabilisation scenario

This annex sketches out a medium-term fiscal stabilisation scenario. Chapter II highlighted the key ingredients to successful macroeconomic stabilisation as being:

- sustained control of the PSBR,
- strict limits on money financing,
- and a return of confidence in the direction of economic policy by reining in inflation.

Medium-term prospects for the economy depend critically on how rapidly these elements can be put into place.

An illustrative fiscal stabilisation scenario is presented below. Its key assumptions are that macroeconomic policies are set to achieve 10 per cent inflation by the year 2000, the debt-to-GDP ratio stabilises at a sustainable level (in line with the Maastricht guidelines), and that progress in microeconomic reform is accelerated. Realising these assumptions is necessary to bring down inflation expectations and risk premia over the next six years. Initial conditions are also critical. This scenario takes the draft 1995 budget targets for tax revenue, and non-interest government expenditure as starting points. Inflation and interest rates have been calibrated to end-1994 developments, to illustrate key pressure points in the coming years.

The main features of the scenario are summarised in Table A4. GDP is projected to be export-led in 1995, with exports growing strongly in response to the 30 per cent real exchange-rate depreciation in 1994 and by stronger export market growth (especially in Europe). Domestic demand is likely to remain subdued as macroeconomic policy remains restrictive. Real interest rates on debt paying market rates (based on "expected" rather than past inflation) are projected to be close to 30 per cent in 1995. This includes a substantial risk premium, due to past failures to achieve announced budget and inflation targets and uncertainty concerning the continuity of sound macroeconomic policy. Inflation is projected to average 70 per cent in 1995, but with the 12-month rate of inflation declining sharply in April, when the large price increases of April 1994 drop out of the 12-month comparison.

Domestic demand growth is expected to pick up from 1996, enabling a more broadly-based recovery, and GDP growth could pick up to 4½ per cent. Nominal interest rates are projected to fall from 80 per cent in 1995 to 50 per cent in 1996 and to around 20 per cent in 2000, as inflation falls and risk premia are steadily reduced. Real interest

Table A4. **Medium-term fiscal stabilisation scenario**

	1993	1994	1995	1996	1997	1998	1999	2000
Real GDP, demand components and inflation (percentage changes)								
Real GDP	7.5	−4.8	2.8	4.5	6.4	6.3	5.7	5.1
Consumer spending	7.1	−4.7	2.0	3.5	5.5	5.8	5.8	5.5
Government spending	4.8	−1.3	−1.4	1.6	3.0	3.0	3.0	3.0
Fixed investment	21.7	−23.7	−2.5	4.3	10.4	10.2	7.6	6.0
Exports	7.7	15.0	15.0	13.0	10.0	9.0	9.0	9.0
Imports	35.8	−20.0	7.5	11.0	11.0	11.0	11.0	10.0
Inflation [1]	63	120	70	40	25	15	12	10
Public sector deficit and debt ratios (as per cent of GDP)								
Consolidated budget	−7.0	−3.6	−6.5	−6.2	−4.9	−4.6	−4.2	−4.1
Other public sector balance	−5.2	−4.3	−0.7	0.0	0.0	0.0	0.0	0.0
PSBR	−12.2	−7.9	−7.2	−6.2	−4.9	−4.6	−4.2	−4.1
Primary balance	−6.2	−0.5	2.0	2.0	2.0	1.0	1.0	1.0
Interest payments	6.1	7.4	9.2	8.2	6.9	5.6	5.2	5.1
Money financed	2.0	1.3	1.0	1.0	0.8	0.6	0.5	0.4
Bond financed	10.2	6.6	6.2	5.1	4.1	4.0	3.7	3.6
Domestic debt [2]	13	15	18	20	19	18	17	17
Total public debt	46	58	51	46	42	41	40	40
Interest rates								
Nominal	72	92	80	50	35	25	22	20
Real [3]	−20	13	29	20	17	12	11	9

1. GDP deflator.
2. Debt-paying market rates of interest (Treasury bonds and bills).
3. Deflated using inflation over following year.
Source: OECD.

rates are assumed to fall from 20 per cent in 1996 to 10 per cent in 2000, providing stimulus for domestic demand and investment. From 1997 onwards, GDP could be growing above its estimated potential growth rate of around 5.0 per cent per annum (see below). The 1994 recession and slow recovery in 1995 will leave a substantial output gap which will maintain downward pressure on inflation, provided that money financing of fiscal deficits remains under tight control, and competitive pressures are enhanced.

Tight control of money creation is a key assumption. Without this, the projected reduction in inflation would not be feasible. It is also assumed that structural reform to broaden the tax base and reduce SEEs deficits will permit a further improvement in the public sector primary balance from a deficit of 0.5 per cent of GDP in 1994 to a surplus of around 2 per cent of GDP between 1995 and 1997. Decisive fiscal consolidation in the next two to three years should help to establish the credibility of the programme and should enable real interest rates to fall. This in turn will permit smaller primary surpluses in later years, reflected here in the assumed decline to surpluses of 1 per cent of GDP after 1998.

How long high interest rates will be necessary to rein in inflation is uncertain. In 1995, high interest rates and the short maturity of government debt is assumed to increase debt interest payments to over 9 per cent of GDP. The decline in the PSBR from 8 per cent in 1994 to 6 per cent in 1996 is thus wholly due to improvements in the primary balance. It is assumed that adherence to the medium-term fiscal strategy will allow interest rates to decline substantially after 1996. Between 1996 and 2000, spending on interest payments are projected to decline by roughly 3 per cent of GDP.

A positive feature of the scenario is that the current account balance and servicing of the foreign debt are unlikely to be constraints (some 67 per cent of Turkey's external debt is at fixed interest rates). No change in the "real exchange rate" is assumed over the next six years for technical reasons. If this assumption is realised, then a regression of the current balance to GDP ratio against the real exchange rate suggests that the current account might remain in surplus of close to 2 per cent of GDP. A real appreciation of around 20 per cent from its September 1994 levels would return the current account to approximate balance, with an estimated standard error of around 0.9 per cent of GDP.[1]

The ratio of foreign-denominated public sector debt to GDP rose sharply from 32 per cent of GDP at the end of 1993 to an estimated 42 per cent at the end of 1994, reflecting the devaluation of the lira. In 1995, foreign debt repayment of US$5.5 billion is projected to be largely domestically financed, with only US$0.5 billion coming from new foreign borrowing. This borrowing schedule would allow the foreign debt-to-GDP ratio to drop back to 33 per cent by the end of 1995, and to 23 per cent of GDP by the end of 1997. By 1998 the public sector could borrow US$8.5 billion a year in foreign currency-denominated debt, while keeping the foreign debt ratio at 23 per cent of GDP between 1998 and 2000. (Indeed, this low foreign debt level would provide the authorities with scope for shifting the mix between foreign and domestic borrowing if needed and/or to accept a limited appreciation of the real exchange rate).

In contrast, the domestic debt to GDP ratio will rise from 13 per cent of GDP at the end of 1993 to 20 per cent of GDP by the end of 1996. This sharp initial increase reflects the fact that almost all public borrowing will be from domestic capital markets in 1994 and 1995, at high nominal and real rates of interest. From 1998 onwards, a primary surplus of 1 per cent of GDP a year is sufficient to gradually lower the domestic debt-to-GDP ratio to around 20 per cent of GDP, and the total public sector debt ratio to 40 per cent by the year 2000.

The scenario indicates that successful fiscal adjustment is possible if primary surpluses of 1 to 2 per cent of GDP are achieved in the next few years. Table A5 shows a sensitivity analysis in which real interest rates are 1 per cent higher and the primary balance is 1 per cent lower from 1995 to 2000 compared to the base case. For simplicity, it is assumed that GDP growth, inflation, and borrowing from foreign markets are the same as in the base case scenario.

In summary, the medium-term scenario and sensitivity analysis highlight the crucial role of attaining primary budget surpluses. Significant fiscal slippage would be costly, because a successful transition from money to debt financing depends critically on

Table A5. **Sensitivity analysis: relative to the base case**

Change in total debt to GDP ratio, percentage points

	1996	1998	2000
Real interest rates higher by 1 percentage point, 1995-2000	0.3	0.6	1.0
Primary balance in greater deficit by 1 percentage point of GDP, 1995-2000	2.0	4.1	6.5

Source: OECD.

building credibility, lowering inflation expectations and risk premia, and reducing uncertainty over the future course of macroeconomic policy. The only way to build policy credibility is to establish a consistent track record of fiscal success. The short maturity structure of government debt is thus a two-edged sword. It heightens the risk of a debt/service spiral and financial market instability in the event of fiscal slippage. Conversely, achieving fiscal targets consistently could put the economy quickly onto a "virtuous circle", as new and existing debt is financed on progressively more favourable terms.

Notes

1. The following regression relates the current-account-to-GDP ratio to the real-exchange rate and to total final expenditure:

$$\text{DCBR} = \underset{(4.4)}{47.8866} - \underset{(6.7)}{1.1433} \text{ CBR } (-1) - \underset{(4.5)}{10.252} \text{ LREXCH } (-1) - \underset{(4.8)}{35.935} \text{ DEVTFE}$$

where:

CBR	= current account balance as per cent GDP,
DCBR	= change in CBR,
LREXCH	= logarithm of the real exchange-rate,
DEVTFE	= deviation of total final expenditure from its long-term trend.

The real exchange rate is an OECD Secretariat measure of trade-weighted exchange rates adjusted for relative consumer price inflation. The equation was estimated using semi-annual data over the period 1982 S1 to 1994 S1.

Figures in brackets are t-ratios of each coefficient. If total final expenditure is at trend, DEVTFE = 0, the equation relates the current-account balance ratio to the level of the real-exchange rate, as follows:

	Real-exchange rate	Current account (% of GDP)
December 1993 level	131.2	−1.8
September 1994 level	87.9	1.7
	106.8	0.0

Potential output growth

This annex assesses the determinants of potential output growth and presents a preliminary estimate of the output gap.[1] One of the key analytical problems in assessing medium-term issues is assessing potential output growth. The analysis below is based on economic developments since the 1980s and makes no allowance for the specific impact of the pending EU customs union on trend productivity. If the experience of the High-Performing Asian Economies serves as a guide, increased foreign and domestic competition will probably boost the growth of potential output. As noted in Annex II, improved supply side prospects will speed the process of fiscal consolidation.

Production-function estimates of trend output

The OECD Secretariat estimates the medium-term trend growth of output in Turkey to be around 4½ per cent per annum. Estimates of the growth of potential output and the output gaps that are derived from them are imprecise, but are representative of recent and prospective trends in the Turkish economy. However, more rapid structural reform and the attainment of low inflation would also favour faster growth of potential output (see below).

The estimates have been derived using a Cobb-Douglas production function[2] with constant returns to total factor inputs. This allows the decomposition of potential output growth into contributions from employment, the capital stock and total factor productivity (TFP).

The relation was:

$$\log(GDP) = \log(TFP) + a*\log(employment) + (1 - a)*\log (capital\ stock)$$

where TFP = total factor productivity and "a" represents the share of wages in total factor incomes, assumed to be $\frac{2}{3}$.[3]

The capital stock is estimated by cumulating past gross investment in machinery and equipment and in non-residential construction, using a perpetual inventory method:

$$Capital\ stock_t = (1 - d)*capital\ stock_{t-1} + investment_t$$

where d is the rate of depreciation (assumed to be 5 per cent per annum for machinery and equipment, and 3 per cent for buildings).[4] Applying these assumptions, the ratio of

Table A6. **Estimates of the capital-output ratio**

	1980	1985	1990	1994
Total capital stock/GDP	2.01	1.88	1.77	2.04
Stock of machinery and equipment/GDP	0.85	0.72	0.72	0.97
Stock of buildings/GDP	1.16	1.16	1.05	1.07

Source: OECD estimates.

the total capital stock to GDP is etimated to have fallen from 2.03 in 1980 to 1.88 in 1990, but recovered to 2.04 in 1994 (largely due to the surge in investment in 1993). The ratios of the stock of machinery and equipment to GDP and the ratio of the stock of buildings to GDP stood at 0.97 and 1.07, respectively, in 1994 (see Table A6).

Trend growth of GDP rose from 3³/₄ per cent per annum in the early 1980s to 4¹/₂ per cent in the late 1980s, with two-thirds of the improvement due to productivity growth and one-third due to the growth of capital stock (Table A7). In the early 1990s, the growth rate of potential output declined to around 4 per cent, with a further contribution of the capital stock being more than offset by a decline in trend TFP (from 2¹/₄ to 1¹/₂ per cent per annum). The OECD projects that structural reform will raise trend TFP in the second half of the 1990s. This, in turn, would raise the growth of potential output from below 4 per cent in 1994 to over 4¹/₂ per cent in 1999-2000 (Diagram A1).

In the 1980s, GDP grew much faster than potential output and, as a consequence, the output gap swung from a negative figure of –5 per cent in 1981 to 3¹/₂ per cent in 1990 (Diagram A2). The output gap reached a positive figure of 4¹/₂ per cent in 1993. In 1994, there has been an estimated 7¹/₂ percentage point decline in actual GDP relative to

Table A7. **The growth of actual and potential output**

	1980-85	1985-90	1990-95	1995-2000
Growth of GDP	4.7	5.3	2.3	5.4
Growth of potential output	3.7	4.5	4.2	4.5
Contributions to potential output growth				
Growth of employment	1.0	0.9	0.7	0.9
Growth of capital stock	1.2	1.4	1.7	1.4
Growth of total factor productivity	1.5	2.2	1.6	2.2

Source: OECD estimates.

Diagram A1. **CONTRIBUTIONS TO TREND OUTPUT GROWTH**

Percentage change over a year earlier

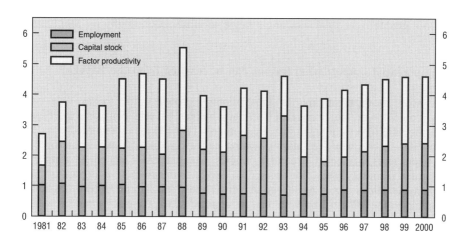

Source: OECD.

Diagram A2. **ESTIMATED OUTPUT GAP**

Per cent of trend GDP[1]

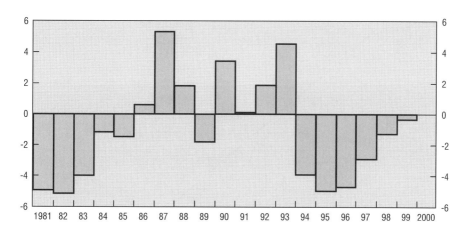

1. Trend GDP estimated by OECD Secretariat.
Source: OECD.

potential GDP, resulting in a negative output gap of –4 per cent. The emergence of a substantial negative output gap implies that there is now significant excess capacity in product markets, for the first time since the early 1980s. This should support disinflation in the next two to three years. The output gap is expected to widen further in 1995 and only close gradually in 1996, but might begin to close more rapidly in 1997.[5]

Raising potential output: what lessons can be learned from the HPAEs?

As noted above, raising the trend rate of output growth from 5 to, say, 7 per cent per annum would lower the financeable primary budget balance considerably. Since the 1960s, the High-Performing Asian Economies (HPAEs) have recorded the highest growth rates in the world economy, against a background of stable macroeconomic policies and market-oriented structural policies. Many HPAEs started growing quickly from poorer resource bases, lower income levels and national saving ratios than in Turkey in the 1960s – raising the issue why Turkey's economic record has not been comparable to the HPAEs and what can be done to raise potential output growth.[6]

The HPAEs "growth-friendly" macro/micro-economic policy mix actively encouraged savings, while favouring investment in physical and human capital, through low budget deficits and inflation. Exports of manufactures were favoured, with import

Diagram A3. **INFLATION AND GDP PER CAPITA GROWTH, 1980-92**

14 middle-income countries

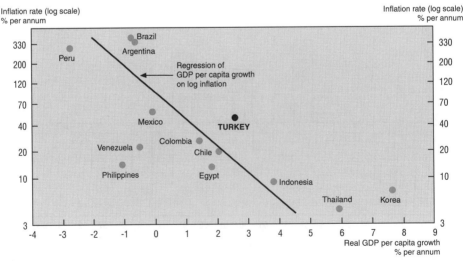

Source: World Bank, *World Tables.*

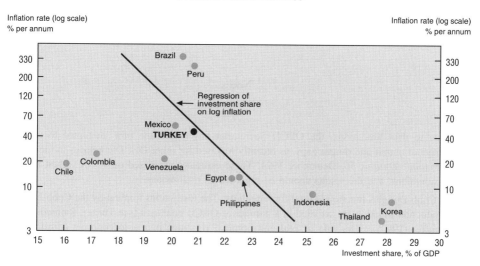

Diagram A4. **INFLATION AND INVESTMENT, 1980-92**
14 middle-income countries

Source: World Bank, *World Tables.*

competition being gradually increased *via* phased reductions in border protection and a progressive easing in capital controls – thereby minimising external constraints to rapid growth. Such policies have been adopted in Turkey only since the 1980s (see Chapter III).

Sustained, non-inflationary medium-term growth depends on achieving macro and microeconomic conditions which are conducive to saving and investment. Among four-teen middle per capita income countries, GDP per capita growth and investment to GDP ratios have tended to be higher in countries with low inflation rates over the period 1980-92 (Diagrams A3 and A4). Notwithstanding an inflation rate averaging close to 50 per cent, Turkish GDP per capita grew at an average rate of 2.8 per cent. Albeit good, this did not match the performance of Korea, Thailand and Indonesia, all of whom had an average inflation rate of below 10 per cent.

A large part of the HPAEs' success was due to phenomenal rates of factor accumula-tion – TFP growth was high but not extraordinary.[7] Cross-country comparisons suggest that Turkey did rather better than expected in relation to its high inflation rate. In the event, concerns that this performance was unsustainable were validated by the early-1994 financial crisis. But now that Turkey is adopting a policy mix conducive to lower budget deficits and is targeting lower inflation and greater public-sector efficiency, this should favour higher domestic savings-investment, and ultimately higher potential output growth.

Notes

1. Due to data limitations, the OECD Secretariat has not in the past attempted to estimate potential output and output gaps, as recently reported for other OECD countries in the *OECD Economic Outlook 56,* December 1994. These estimates are based on strong, albeit realistic assumptions, and the results should be regarded as preliminary.

2. A Cobb-Douglas function is used for simplicity. The restrictions implied by the Cobb-Douglas production function are satisfied in a number of OECD countries (see Turner, Richardson and Rauffet (1993), "The role of real and nominal rigidities in macroeconomic adjustment: a comparative study of the G-3 economies", *OECD Economic Studies,* pp. 87-136, Winter. For Turkey, formal tests of the restrictions are not possible due to the absence of reliable data on factor incomes.

3. Data on factor incomes are not sufficient to provide a reliable estimate of labour-income share. But this income share appears to be close to $2/3$ in most OECD countries, see Englander, Steven, and Andrew Gurney (1994), "OECD Productivity growth: medium-term trends", *OECD Economic Studies,* No. 22, Spring.

4. These assumptions give half-lives of 14 years for machinery and equipment, 23 years for buildings.

5. It is assumed that the output gap will return to around zero by the year 2000.

6. For a comparison between economic development in Turkey and Korea see A.O. Kreueger (1987), "The Importance of Economic Policy in Development: Contrasts between Korea and Turkey", *NBER Working Paper* No. 2195, March, and OECD, *1993/94 Economic Survey of Korea,* Paris.

7. Analysis of TFP in Hong Kong, Singapore, South Korea and Taiwan shows that the extraordinary sustained growth of per capita output was strongly aided by high factor accumulation. TFP growth was high but not remarkable. From 1966 to 1990, TFP growth averaged 2.3 per cent in Hong Kong, –0.3 per cent in Singapore, 1.6 per cent in South Korea and 1.9 per cent in Taiwan. This implies that the phenomenal growth process in Asia can be explained by conventional economic theory. See Alwyn Young (1994), "The Tyranny of Numbers: Confronting the Statistical Realities of the East-Asian Growth Experience", *NBER Working Paper No. 4680,* p. 33. See also the *World Bank* (1993), "The East-Asian Miracle".

Annex V

Calendar of main economic events

1994

January

In the course of unusual unrest in financial and foreign exchange markets, the Turkish lira depreciates by 13.6 per cent.

Central Bank rediscount rate is revised from 48 to 50 per cent and advance rate from 54.5 to 65 per cent.

The legal reserve requirement and the liquidity ratio are unified to a single "liquidity requirement ratio" and its coverage extended to non-deposit liabilities. Previously, the reserve requirement ratios on Turkish lira deposits were 16 per cent for sight deposits and 7.5 per cent for time deposits. For foreign exchange deposits reserve requirement had to be held both in foreign exchange and in Turkish lira. The liquidity requirement ratio was 35 per cent on total deposits, but banks were allowed to hold 70 per cent in interest-bearing government paper. The new "liquidity requirement ratio" is 22 per cent on all liabilities except sight deposits, but including asset-backed investment funds and mutual-investment funds. Of the 22 per cent liquidity requirement 6 percentage points have to be held in Turkish lira, 3 percentage points in foreign currency and 13 percentage points in interest-bearing government paper.

Downgrading of credit-rating on sovereign Turkish debt to below investment grade paper by Standard and Poor's and Moody's.

February

Suspension of 5 per cent transaction tax on government bonds and on repo transactions, which was introduced in January 1994.

New liquidity ratio, which was introduced in January, is also suspended.

The Turkish lira depreciates 17 per cent (trade-weighted index).

March

Acceleration in depreciation of the lira during the month.

Local elections on 27 March.

April

Average value of the lira 62 per cent lower than in March. Lira falls to a low of 39 900 TL/$US on 7 April, but recovers to 33 400 TL/$US by end of month.

Announcement of 5 April stabilisation programme. Immediate price increases of 70 to 100 per cent for State economic enterprises, to be followed by a six-month freeze. Consolidated budget deficit for 1994 to be reduced from TL 198 trillion to TL 103 trillion. One-third of deficit reduction to come from one-time taxes on net assets of firms, wealth of individuals and on personal and corporate tax surcharges. Spending measures included a freeze on public sector wages, reduced transfers to State economic enterprises (SEEs), and reduced investment spending. Measures to speed structural reforms, to include accelerating privatisation programme, closure of major loss-making public enterprises, and improved tax administration.

New law regarding Central Bank advances to Treasury. Permitted Central Bank advances to be reduced from 15 per cent of budget appropriations in 1994, to 12 per cent in 1995, 10 per cent in 1996, 6 per cent in 1997, and 3 per cent from 1998 onwards.

Revision of reserve and liquidity requirements to enhance prudential control of banking system, and to increase attractiveness of holding Turkish lira rather than foreign currency deposits. Reserve and liquidity ratios to apply to eleven bank liabilities (asset-backed securities as well as deposits). Ratios to apply to Investment Banks and Special Finance Institutions. Reserve requirements changed to 10 per cent on foreign exchange deposits and 8 per cent on Turkish lira deposits.

As a result of exchange-rate depreciation and SEE price rises, the monthly rise in April wholesale prices jumps to 33 per cent, taking twelve-month inflation rate to 125 per cent.

Central Bank guarantees 100 per cent of bank deposits, following the placing of three small banks into receivership.

May

Stabilisation of Turkish lira.

Treasury resumes borrowing from domestic capital markets by issuing four tranches of TL 10 trillion "Superbonds", yielding simple interest of 50 per cent over three months.

June

Budget surplus of TL 9.3 trillion in April-June period, well within stabilisation programme target of TL 10 trillion deficit.

July

IMF approves a stand-by arrangement of $US742 million, over 14-month period. Constitutional court annuls decrees authorising fast-track privatisation.

August

Standard and Poor's remove Turkey from creditwatch.

September

April-September target for consolidated budget borrowing is achieved (borrowing of TL 13 trillion, compared with target of TL 35 trillion).

October

New law allows creditors to sequestrate the assets of State economic enterprises and municipalities in the event of non-payment of debts.

Draft 1995 budget presented to Parliament. Revised estimate of TL 139 trillion for 1994 consolidated budget deficit, and planned deficit of TL 198 trillion for 1995.

Interest-rates on 3-month Treasury bills reach post-April low of 19.3 per cent a quarter, but Treasury accepts higher interest rates in subsequent auctions.

November

New privatisation law passed by Parliament. Privatisation Administration envisages sales of $US5 billion in 1995.

Turkey resumes borrowing on foreign capital markets, with $US352 million loan with a guarantee from the US Ex-Im Bank.

Postponement of Parliamentary bye-elections scheduled for 4 December.

Supplementary budget for 1994 of TL 100 trillion approved by Parliament.

December

1995 budget approved by Parliament with minor revisions.
Anti-cartel legislation approved by Parliament.

STATISTICAL ANNEX AND STRUCTURAL INDICATORS

Table A. **Gross domestic product, current prices**

TL billion

	1984	1985	1986	1987	1988	1989	1990	1991	1992	1993
Private consumption	16 626	24 930	34 394	51 019	82 050	149 140	269 562	434 366	734 306	1 289 008
Government consumption	1 964	3 139	4 592	5 845	9 837	21 240	43 083	78 256	141 318	254 889
Gross fixed capital investment	4 168	7 650	12 745	18 491	33 738	51 837	89 892	149 272	251 435	484 588
Construction	2 228	4 285	6 354	11 727	22 559	36 103	57 388	95 425	159 138	280 377
Non-housing	1 611	3 078	3 585	5 392	8 700	14 672	23 555	40 694	66 343	110 170
Housing	617	1 207	2 769	6 335	13 859	21 431	33 833	54 731	92 795	170 207
Machinery and equipment	1 940	3 365	6 391	6 764	11 179	15 734	32 504	53 847	92 297	204 211
Increase in stocks	-87	136	409	687	-1 247	1 522	6 601	-6 160	4 000	21 619
Total domestic demand	29 067	47 790	71 239	106 260	180 675	311 679	556 418	900 431	1 541 632	2 815 069
Exports of goods and services	3 574	5 762	7 043	11 642	24 106	36 833	52 215	87 215	157 360	270 997
Imports of goods and services	4 248	6 522	8 104	13 267	22 682	40 420	69 042	104 819	189 646	383 358
Statistical discrepancy	0	0	0	306	3 424	7 172	749	-8 013	-5 405	-24 593
Gross domestic product	21 997	35 095	51 079	74 723	129 226	227 324	393 060	630 117	1 093 368	1 913 150

Note: In this annex, all GDP data refer to the new series of the National Accounts as published by the State Institute of Statistics.
Source: State Institute of Statistics, *Gross National Product*, and OECD, *National Accounts*.

Table B. **Gross domestic product, constant prices**

1987 prices, TL billion

	1984	1985	1986	1987	1988	1989	1990	1991	1992	1993
Private consumption	48 654	48 358	51 179	51 018	51 638	51 105	57 803	58 913	60 864	65 168
Government consumption	4 284	4 889	5 341	5 845	5 783	5 830	6 297	6 579	6 828	7 159
Gross fixed capital investment	10 547	11 756	12 742	18 491	18 299	18 701	21 670	21 935	22 882	27 843
Construction	7 494	8 677	8 778	11 727	11 688	12 331	12 543	12 289	12 830	13 306
Non-housing	5 551	6 158	4 814	5 392	4 528	5 037	5 336	5 206	5 354	5 148
Housing	1 943	2 519	3 964	6 335	7 160	7 294	7 207	7 083	7 476	8 158
Machinery and equipment	3 053	3 079	3 964	6 764	6 611	6 370	9 127	9 646	10 052	14 537
Increase in stocks	–228	248	563	687	–693	520	1 513	–939	402	1 486
Total domestic demand	63 257	65 251	69 825	76 041	75 027	76 156	87 283	86 488	90 976	101 656
Exports of goods and services	9 898	9 707	9 212	11 642	13 786	13 751	14 102	14 627	16 236	17 484
Imports of goods and services	11 975	11 183	10 788	13 267	12 670	13 543	18 014	17 074	18 938	25 715
Statistical discrepancy	0	0	0	306	163	134	208	312	1 127	2 665
Gross domestic product	61 180	63 775	68 249	74 722	76 306	76 498	83 579	84 353	89 401	96 090

Source: State Institute of Statistics, *Gross National Product,* and OECD, *National Accounts.*

Table C. **Gross domestic product by kind of activity**

TL billion

	1985	1986	1987	1988	1989	1990	1991	1992	1993
	Current prices								
Agriculture, forestry, fishing	6 910	9 967	13 314	22 303	37 704	68 692	96 074	163 827	275 146
Mining	561	829	1 475	2 357	4 625	6 269	9 762	14 946	21 814
Manufacturing	6 407	11 340	16 319	29 664	52 561	86 307	139 709	236 573	412 408
Electricity, gas and water	636	838	1 482	2 829	4 408	7 745	13 839	28 602	51 450
Construction	2 052	3 545	5 452	9 998	15 904	24 746	44 139	74 509	135 753
Wholesale and retail trade, restaurants and hotels	6 691	9 330	14 850	25 699	42 653	74 912	117 433	202 369	359 361
Transport, storage and communication	4 461	5 955	8 660	15 245	26 317	46 490	74 561	133 338	227 785
Financial institutions	3 304	4 695	6 672	10 137	14 889	25 878	49 287	84 708	146 669
Community, social and personal services	827	1 207	1 736	3 198	7 544	14 415	23 006	39 577	68 707
Producers of government services	1 788	2 394	3 789	6 363	15 535	32 525	61 051	111 841	203 922
Imputed bank service change	-327	729	1 997	3 349	2 562	9 838	23 282	41 188	77 108
Import duties	984	1 504	2 652	4 246	6 854	13 397	22 206	40 713	81 229
Gross domestic product at factor cost	35 095	51 079	74 722	129 225	227 324	393 060	630 117	1 093 368	1 913 150
	Percentage volume change, 1987 prices								
Agriculture, forestry, fishing	-0.5	4.6	0.4	7.8	-7.6	6.8	-0.9	4.3	-2.2
Mining	11.6	14.4	2.5	-4.6	13.0	-2.5	4.5	0.3	-6.4
Manufacturing	5.7	10.5	10.1	1.6	3.0	9.7	2.4	5.8	9.3
Electricity, gas and water	6.8	13.7	5.8	10.4	13.9	8.6	4.5	11.8	8.9
Construction	13.6	11.0	14.9	-5.4	6.1	-1.1	1.1	6.2	6.9
Wholesale and retail trade, restaurants and hotels	5.6	4.8	19.0	3.5	-2.3	12.3	-0.7	6.9	11.3
Transport, storage and communication	-1.4	2.7	10.2	1.2	3.2	11.9	-0.4	8.1	8.7
Financial institutions	1.9	2.9	3.6	1.6	2.6	2.3	1.8	0.9	1.7
Community, social and personal services	3.6	6.5	9.1	2.3	0.3	8.1	0.9	5.5	6.3
Producers of government services	2.8	2.6	-0.2	1.9	1.2	2.9	2.4	3.4	1.6
Imputed bank service change	2.3	4.1	3.8	4.1	2.1	1.9	0.2	-2.3	-0.6
Import duties	42.8	37.8	28.2	-10.3	-2.6	48.3	4.1	11.3	32.8
Gross domestic product at factor cost	4.2	7.0	9.5	2.1	0.3	9.3	0.9	6.0	7.5

Source: State Institute of Statistics, *Gross National Product*, and OECD, *National Accounts*.

Table D. **Industrial production**

Percentage changes, volume

Index 1986=100, value-added weighted

	1987	1988	1989	1990	1991	1992	1993	1994		
								Q1	Q2	Q3
Total industry	**10.5**	**1.7**	**3.6**	**9.5**	**2.6**	**5.0**	**8.4**	**6.0**	**-8.7**	**-8.7**
Public	12.8	3.0	0.9	7.9	3.9	3.8	6.1	7.3	6.8	1.7
Private	8.7	0.5	6.0	10.6	1.6	6.0	10.2	5.2	-19.7	-16.7
Mining	**5.1**	**-5.2**	**12.6**	**6.0**	**10.1**	**-3.0**	**-8.7**	**1.4**	**7.7**	**-2.6**
Energy	**11.7**	**8.4**	**8.1**	**10.8**	**3.8**	**12.2**	**10.0**	**8.8**	**6.1**	**4.7**
Manufacturing	**10.7**	**1.0**	**2.1**	**9.5**	**1.8**	**4.2**	**9.3**	**5.7**	**-12.6**	**-12.0**
Public	14.1	2.0	-5.5	5.5	1.6	1.2	6.9	7.5	4.9	-0.5
Private	9.0	0.4	6.5	11.6	1.9	5.7	10.5	4.9	-20.1	-17.1
By manufacturing sector										
Foods, beverages, tobacco	3.5	4.5	6.7	6.8	9.2	-3.6	6.0	16.9	4.0	-7.4
Textile, clothing, leather	8.4	1.9	3.1	2.3	-8.6	4.3	4.3	7.3	-14.0	-10.4
Wood and cork products	4.4	-2.8	2.0	17.4	-6.2	0.6	-0.7	14.8	-15.2	-29.7
Paper and printing	14.2	-7.3	2.6	15.3	-5.9	9.8	5.2	1.8	-7.8	-8.0
Chemicals, petroleum	15.2	2.7	0.4	3.3	-0.6	3.2	7.9	1.2	-9.9	-5.2
Non-metallic mineral products	13.0	6.1	4.8	3.8	4.6	11.7	2.4	22.0	-6.5	-6.6
Basic metal industry	12.2	-0.2	1.3	16.8	-7.8	6.5	11.1	7.5	-2.8	-0.1
Machinery and transport equipment	8.5	-6.7	-1.2	31.8	12.0	8.1	20.5	0.5	-32.4	-33.6
Other manufacturing	11.4	-17.4	72.9	34.3	-22.7	40.7	-10.9	-31.7	-23.6	-33.5

Source: State Institute of Statistics, *Quarterly Industrial Production Index.*

Table E. **Prices**[1]

Annual percentage changes

	Wholesale prices							Consumer prices	
	General index			Agriculture	Manufacturing			General	Food
	Total	Public	Private		Mining	Industry	Energy		
				Base year 1981 = 100, 1981 weights				Base year 1978-79 = 100	
Old series (weights)	(100)	(28.55)	(71.45)	(30.39)	(2.98)	(64.25)	(2.38)	(100)	(45.30)
1982	27.0	28.8	26.3	24.5	49.3	26.5	45.7	34.1	29.7
1983	30.5	27.3	31.7	31.2	20.5	31.2	25.7	31.4	26.0
1984	50.3	47.7	51.4	57.5	41.2	46.5	75.3	48.4	57.1
1985	43.2	53.8	39.1	37.4	63.9	41.9	97.6	45.0	40.6
1986	29.6	27.6	30.4	25.3	13.6	32.6	35.6	34.6	30.4
1987	32.0	23.1	35.8	29.6	35.7	33.6	23.4	38.9	39.8
1988	68.3	68.9	68.1	51.0	70.0	77.8	40.2	75.4	71.1
1989	69.6	67.9	70.2	81.4	84.1	64.6	66.0	69.6	70.6
				Base year 1987 = 100, 1987 weights				Base year 1987 = 100	
New series (weights)	(100)	(27.74)	(72.26)	(23.03)	(2.54)	(69.80)	(4.62)	(100)	(32.10)
1988	70.5	70.3	70.5	44.1	64.1	81.5	40.9	73.7	83.2
1989	64.0	64.2	63.9	71.7	65.0	61.6	69.2	63.2	69.3
1990	52.3	56.7	50.6	70.6	48.7	46.9	56.5	60.3	64.3
1991	55.3	61.3	53.0	50.8	63.2	55.3	75.1	66.0	67.1
1992	62.1	65.2	60.8	62.7	61.6	55.3	97.7	70.1	71.3
1993	58.4	54.5	60.1	62.2	56.7	56.6	67.8	66.1	63.5
1994	120.7	122.5	119.8	97.8	132.8	129.4	102.3	106.3	110.0
1994 Q1	67.8	63.0	69.7	70.6	67.3	66.8	69.2	72.1	72.5
Q2	133.9	149.3	127.7	94.1	146.4	148.0	119.7	113.8	120.2
Q3	128.3	132.2	126.5	91.4	157.8	140.2	117.0	109.5	107.4
Q4	141.3	135.0	144.0	126.3	145.7	149.8	99.4	120.6	129.9

1. In January 1990, the State Institute of Statistics introduced new weights for both wholesale and consumer prices indices, and shifted the base year of the consumer price index from 1978-79 to 1987. In January 1991, the base year for the wholesale index was changed from 1981 to 1987.

Source: State Institute of Statistics, *Wholesale and Consumer Price Indices Monthly Bulletin*.

Table F. **Imports by commodities**
$ million

SITC classification	1984	1985	1986	1987	1988	1989	1990	1991	1992	1993
0. Food and live animals	347	289	261	369	180	697	1 179	466	594	839
1. Beverages and tobacco	27	58	125	192	189	225	346	381	330	336
2. Crude materials, inedible, except fuels	588	642	834	1 322	1 353	1 602	1 680	1 614	1 872	2 489
3. Mineral fuels, lubricants and related materials	3 795	3 786	2 192	3 172	3 062	3 258	4 641	3 773	3 782	3 990
4. Animal and vegetable oils, fats and waxes	231	215	141	145	227	307	297	393	375	403
5. Chemicals and related products, n.e.s.	1 551	1 473	1 585	2 146	2 215	2 321	2 830	2 852	3 092	3 527
6. Manufactured goods classified chiefly by material	1 233	1 508	1 512	2 341	2 436	2 795	3 372	3 295	3 606	5 026
7. Machinery and transport equipment	2 683	3 055	4 035	4 054	4 234	4 095	7 030	7 168	8 043	11 228
8. Miscellanous manufactured articles	207	249	327	421	442	485	905	990	1 105	1 461
9. Commodities and transactions not classified elsewhere	0	0	9	1	2	4	22	114	73	131
Total	10 663	11 275	11 020	14 163	14 340	15 789	22 302	21 047	22 871	29 429

Source: OECD, *Foreign Trade by Commodities*, Series C.

Table G. **Exports by commodities**
$ million

SITC classification	1984	1985	1986	1987	1988	1989	1990	1991	1992	1993
0. Food and live animals	1 919	1 594	1 864	2 163	2 484	2 015	2 302	2 728	2 760	2 794
1. Beverages and tobacco	221	337	278	324	278	493	455	593	356	466
2. Crude materials, inedible, except fuels	615	619	604	517	777	837	750	681	503	555
3. Mineral fuels, lubricants and related materials	413	377	185	238	335	260	298	292	235	178
4. Animal and vegetable oils, fats and waxes	45	68	80	83	86	153	139	197	215	187
5. Chemicals and related products, n.e.s.	196	298	410	675	950	936	745	603	629	609
6. Manufactured goods classified chiefly by material	1 985	2 617	2 206	2 669	3 503	3 391	3 841	3 717	4 155	4 485
7. Machinery and transport equipment	353	645	415	1 085	748	587	853	1 016	1 290	1 292
8. Miscellanous manufactured articles	1 366	1 387	1 400	2 411	2 497	2 949	3 567	3 758	4 561	4 775
9. Commodities and transactions not classified elsewhere	19	15	15	24	4	7	7	8	10	9
Total	7 134	7 958	7 457	10 190	11 662	11 627	12 957	13 593	14 715	15 349

Source: OECD, *Foreign Trade by Commodities*, Series C.

Table H. Geographic distribution of foreign trade
$ million, monthly averages

	Imports						Exports					
	1988	1989	1990	1991	1992	1993	1988	1989	1990	1991	1992	1993
OECD countries	9 251	9 934	14 251	14 072	15 423	19 975	6 737	7 201	8 821	8 857	9 346	9 072
EU countries	5 908	6 076	9 354	9 223	10 049	12 950	5 128	5 432	6 904	7 042	7 601	7 293
of which: France	829	745	1 340	1 227	1 351	1 952	499	595	737	689	809	771
Germany	2 067	2 225	3 523	3 232	3 754	4 533	2 178	2 196	3 076	3 413	3 660	3 654
Italy	1 006	1 071	1 727	1 845	1 919	2 558	955	978	1 106	972	943	750
United Kingdom	739	728	1 014	1 166	1 187	1 546	576	616	744	676	796	835
Other OECD countries	3 343	3 858	4 897	4 849	5 375	7 025	1 609	1 769	1 917	1 815	1 746	1 780
of which: Japan	555	530	1 120	1 092	1 113	1 621	209	233	239	226	162	158
Switzerland	344	412	537	489	688	651	265	174	293	246	223	216
United States	1 520	2 094	2 282	2 255	2 601	3 351	761	971	968	913	865	986
Central and eastern European countries	857	1 124	1 947	1 875	2 094	3 253	520	923	829	1 053	1 217	1 670
Middle East and North Africa	2 841	2 830	3 659	2 981	3 238	3 240	3 456	2 804	2 452	2 694	2 763	2 743
of which: Iran	660	233	492	91	365	667	546	561	495	487	455	290
Iraq	1 441	1 650	1 047	0	1	0	986	445	215	122	212	160
Kuwait	89	81	54	0	68	84	199	168	92	16	66	104
Libya	79	286	487	281	445	131	218	227	221	237	247	246
Saudi Arabia	229	212	724	1 829	1 665	1 500	359	365	338	485	486	652
Other countries	1 391	1 902	2 445	2 119	2 116	2 962	949	699	856	990	1 388	1 863
Total	14 340	15 790	22 302	21 047	22 871	29 429	11 662	11 627	12 957	13 593	14 715	15 349

Source: OECD, Monthly Statistics of Foreign Trade, Series A.

99

Table I. Balance of payments
$ million

	1985	1986	1987	1988	1989	1990	1991	1992	1993
Exports	8 255	7 583	10 322	11 929	11 780	13 026	13 667	14 892	15 610
Imports	11 230	10 664	13 551	13 706	15 999	22 581	21 007	23 082	29 772
Trade balance	-2 975	-3 081	-3 229	-1 777	-4 219	-9 555	-7 340	-8 190	-14 162
Services	-22	-308	33	1 214	1 622	2 437	2 499	3 189	4 014
Balance of goods and services	-2 997	-3 389	-3 196	-563	-2 597	-7 118	-4 827	-5 001	-10 148
Private transfers, net	1 762	1 703	2 066	1 827	3 135	3 349	2 854	3 147	3 035
Official transfers, net	222	221	324	332	423	1 144	2 245	912	733
Current balance	-1 013	-1 465	-806	1 596	961	-2 625	258	-942	-6 380
Long-term capital	262	1 312	1 841	1 323	1 364	1 037	623	2 252	5 909
Private, net	856	1 157	1 388	2 037	2 456	1 847	1 562	3 351	6 839
Official, net	-594	155	453	-714	-1 092	-810	-939	-1 099	-930
Basic balance	-751	-153	1 035	2 919	2 325	-1 588	881	1 310	-471
Non-monetary short-term private capital, net	463	447	-542	-351	23	1 362	37	1 641	1 850
Non-monetary short-term official capital, net	158	-302	305	-895	-526	359	-322	136	133
Errors and omissions	-837	-118	-506	515	971	-468	926	-1 222	-2 275
Balance on non-monetary transactions	-967	-126	292	2 188	2 793	-335	1 540	1 865	-763
Private monetary institutions short-term capital	858	667	287	-1 035	-81	1 279	-2 735	-381	1 071
Assets	382	-93	-434	-1 046	-370	-769	-2 595	-2 474	-3 231
Liabilities	476	760	721	11	289	2 048	-140	2 093	4 302
Net transactions of monetary authorities	-109	541	579	1 153	2 712	944	-1 199	1 484	308
Use of IMF credit	-251	-377	-443	-432	-238	-48	0	0	0
Miscellaneous official accounts	-1	-1	1	1	-3	-1	2	0	0
Allocation of SDR's	0	0	0	0	0	0	0	0	0
Change in reserves	-361	163	137	722	2 471	895	-1 197	1 484	308
Gold	0	0	0	0	-14	114	25	0	-6
Currency assets	-360	163	137	721	2 485	781	-1 223	1 484	314
Reserve position in IMF	0	0	0	0	0	0	0	0	0
Special drawing rights	-1	0	0	1	0	0	1	0	0

Source: OECD.

Table J. **External trade indicators**

		Effective exchange rate	Terms of trade	Goods and services	
	Exchange rate TL per $			Exports	Imports
		1987 = 100		1987 prices, TL billion	
1980	76.0	1 057.7	101.7	3 184	7 024
1981	110.2	830.2	101.8	5 205	7 902
1982	160.7	638.4	101.8	6 976	8 554
1983	223.7	487.3	101.8	7 891	10 002
1984	363.5	332.2	101.8	9 898	11 975
1985	519.6	250.5	101.8	9 707	11 183
1986	669.0	156.0	101.8	9 212	10 788
1987	854.6	100.0	100.0	11 642	13 269
1988	1 419.4	59.1	97.7	13 786	12 670
1989	2 120.0	42.0	89.8	13 750	13 543
1990	2 606.5	31.4	96.6	14 102	18 014
1991	4 168.9	20.1	97.1	14 627	17 074
1992	6 860.6	11.9	101.1	16 236	18 938
1993	10 965.6	8.1	100.0	17 484	25 715
1994	29 778.2	3.2	..	..	..
1994 Q1	17 818.6	5.1	104.2	4 551	6 155
Q2	32 934.6	2.7	106.8	4 747	4 460
Q3	32 251.4	2.6	3.9	5 597	4 594
Q4	36 108.1	2.3	..	..	..

Source: OECD, *National Accounts* and *Main Economic Indicators.*

Table K. External debt of Turkey[1]
Disbursed debt – End of period
$ million

	1985	1986	1987	1988	1989	1990	1991	1992	1993	1994 June
Medium- and long-term debt	20 717	25 752	32 605	34 305	36 006	39 536	41 372	42 932	48 823	53 360
Multilateral organisations	6 309	7 839	9 802	9 192	8 740	9 564	10 069	9 160	8 674	8 967
IMF	1 326	1 085	770	299	48	0	0	0	0	0
World Bank, IDA, IFC	3 661	4 917	6 550	6 421	6 137	6 435	6 540	5 761	5 440	5 534
European Investment Bank	453	571	675	583	561	604	602	463	250	260
European Resettlement Fund	815	1 216	1 757	1 836	1 918	2 439	2 859	2 880	2 952	3 144
Islamic Development Bank	12	12	15	22	51	68	54	40	15	13
OPEC Fund	35	30	25	20	15	10	5	3	2	1
International Fund for Agricultural Development		8	10	11	10	8	9	13	15	15
Bilateral credits	8 122	9 646	11 680	11 382	11 431	12 984	14 587	15 035	18 153	20 241
OECD countries	6 647	8 049	10 086	10 038	9 992	11 652	13 169	13 542	16 607	18 699
OPEC countries	915	1 013	1 066	886	697	564	438	363	317	292
Other countries	560	584	528	458	742	768	980	1 130	1 229	1 250
Commercial banks	4 159	4 969	6 391	8 891	10 269	10 721	10 992	12 956	15 706	16 780
Private lenders	2 127	3 298	4 732	4 840	5 566	6 267	5 724	5 781	6 290	7 372
Dresdner Bank scheme	1 858	3 069	4 569	4 723	5 500	6 255	5 713	5 771	6282	7363
Short-term debt	4 759	6 349	7 623	6 417	5 745	9 500	9 117	12 660	18 533	13 221
Commercial banks	1 495	2 673	3 725	2 950	1 841	3 845	4 144	6 490	9 526	5 176
Private lenders	3 264	3 676	3 898	3 467	3 904	5 655	4 973	6 170	9 007	8 045
Foreign exchange deposits	1 562	1986	2 619	2 433	2 795	3 976	2 982	2 594	3 097	3 155
Total debt	25 476	32 101	40 228	40 722	41 751	49 036	50 489	55 592	67 356	66 581
Memorandum items (per cent)										
Total debt/GDP	37.7	42.0	46.1	44.8	39.0	32.5	33.4	35.0	38.7	
Medium- and long-term debt/GDP	30.7	33.7	37.4	37.7	33.6	26.2	27.4	27.0	28.0	
Short-term debt/GDP	7.0	8.3	8.7	7.1	5.4	6.3	6.0	8.0	10.6	
Short-term debt/total debt	18.7	19.8	18.9	15.8	13.8	19.4	18.1	22.8	27.5	
Total debt/foreign exchange revenues	193.2	255.8	237.6	202.3	185.8	185.2	179.6	189.1	215.7	
Total debt by borrower										
General government	50.4	51.3	52.3	56.8	57.3	52.2	54.3	51.2	45.7	
SEEs	8.3	9.2	9.2	9.8	9.9	12.6	10.2	9.2	8.1	
Central Bank	26.4	23.7	23.9	20.6	18.9	16.6	14.0	12.1	10.8	
Private sector	14.9	15.8	14.6	12.8	13.9	18.6	21.5	27.5	35.4	

1. The Turkish authorities have issued a new series of external debt statistics, starting from 1984. Revised series reflect the adjustment for valuation changes in World Bank loans arising from the World Bank's currency pool system and the reclassification of the Dresdner Bank accounts according to maturities. Foreign Military Sales (FMS) refinancing credits are also included. In 1988, $1503 million and in 1989 $403 million FMS loans were rescheduled by a group of US bank under US Treasury guarantee. Other military debt is excluded.

Source: Data provided by the Under-Secretariat of the Treasury and the Foreign Trade, and Central Bank of Turkey.

Table L. Money and banking

TL billion, end of period

	1986	1987	1988	1989	1990	1991	1992	1993
Money supply								
Notes and coins	1 302	2 212	3 426	6 840	11 378	17 449	30 389	51 645
Sight deposits	3 953	6 417	7 886	12 718	20 020	29 344	47 952	77 442
M1	5 255	8 629	11 312	19 558	31 398	46 793	78 341	129 087
Time deposits	6 918	9 019	15 883	27 582	40 172	70 325	112 395	153 355
M2	12 173	17 648	27 194	47 139	71 570	117 118	190 736	282 442
Foreign exchange deposits	2 436	5 356	9 512	14 135	21 793	50 936	103 234	190 617
M2Y	14 609	23 004	36 707	61 274	93 363	168 054	293 970	473 059
Central Bank								
Total assets	14 020	22 322	38 362	48 988	60 987	96 789	177 244	285 801
Foreign assets	3 301	4 778	11 429	17 948	25 583	38 736	75 758	128 126
Domestic assets	10 719	17 544	26 933	31 040	35 404	58 053	101 486	157 675
Cash credits	4 624	7 524	10 039	10 892	10 644	28 199	72 044	127 344
Credit to public sector	3 887	5 607	7 020	7 860	5 324	22 904	62 602	108 482
Credit to private sector	737	1 917	3 019	3 032	5 320	5 295	9 442	18 862
Other items	146	212	−287	−1 058	−1 648	−2 575	−5 293	−1 593
Devaluation account	5 949	9 809	17 181	21 206	26 408	32 429	34 735	31 924
Total liabilities	14 020	22 322	38 362	48 988	60 987	96 789	177 244	285 801
Reserve money	3 999	5 503	10 143	17 035	23 871	37 244	61 195	101 721
Monetary base	4 037	5 993	11 349	17 365	22 944	42 828	82 974	123 556
Central bank money	4 297	6 430	11 852	18 528	23 837	43 993	87 837	128 113
Foreign currency liabilities	9 724	15 892	26 511	30 460	37 150	52 796	89 407	157 688
Deposit money banks								
Deposits[1]	15 595	23 898	38 013	61 648	93 931	164 669	296 151	522 500
Credits	10 219	16 439	23 871	39 357	69 287	106 491	195 182	363 026
Total bank credits (net of Central Bank advances to banks)	13 031	20 133	29 012	43 580	74 659	130 796	244 420	453 771
Central bank	1 942	2 644	3 509	3 506	4 449	18 454	42 584	82 936
Deposit money banks	10 042	16 024	22 769	36 522	65 198	101 452	185 419	342 182
Investment banks	1 047	1 465	2 734	3 552	5 012	10 890	16 418	28 653

1. Including interbank and foreign currency deposits.
Source: Central Bank of Turkey, *Quarterly Bulletin.*

Table M. **Public sector borrowing**

	1986	1987	1988	1989	1990	1991	1992	1993
Public sector deficit (TL billion)	-1 869	-4 563	-6 235	-12 283	-30 933	-67 529	-123 456	-240 944
General government	-549	-2 093	-3 430	-7 863	-14 338	-43 944	-74 214	-171 633
State economic enterprises (SEEs)	-1 320	-2 470	-2 805	-4 420	-14 986	-23 585	-49 242	-69 311
Public sector deficit/GDP	-3.7	-6.1	-4.8	-5.3	-7.8	-10.6	-11.2	-12.5
General government	-1.1	-2.8	-2.7	-3.4	-3.6	-6.9	-6.7	-8.9
Central government	-3.0	-3.5	-3.0	-3.3	-3.0	-5.3	-4.3	-6.9
Local administrations	-0.2	-0.5	-0.4	-0.2	-0.0	-0.3	-0.8	-0.8
Revolving funds	0.3	0.6	0.2	0.4	0.3	-0.1	-0.2	-0.6
Extra-budgetary funds[1]	1.8	0.5	0.5	-0.2	-0.8	-1.2	-1.4	-0.5
SEEs[2]	-2.6	-3.3	-2.2	-1.9	-4.2	-3.7	-4.5	-3.6
Sources of financing (per cent of total)								
Central Bank	14.1	20.4	15.8	3.7	1.5	16.5	15.0	17.2
Foreign borrowing, net	58.0	44.2	43.3	15.5	12.7	3.3	14.0	4.9
Domestic borrowing, net[3]	27.9	35.4	40.9	80.8	85.8	80.2	71.0	77.9
Memorandum items								
Public debt/GDP								
General government	42.0	47.7	47.3	39.9	31.5	33.1	35.0	36.8
Domestic	21.3	24.3	22.8	18.7	14.7	15.1	17.2	19.3
Foreign	20.7	23.4	24.5	21.2	16.8	18.0	17.8	17.5
SEEs								
Domestic	n.a.	n.a.	n.a.	n.a.	n.a.	n.a.	n.a.	n.a.
Foreign	3.8	4.2	4.4	4.0	3.1	3.4	3.2	3.1

1. Including State economic enterprises in the process of privatisation.
2. Including non-financial SEEs.
3. Including short-term borrowing.
Source: Undersecretariat of Treasury and Foreign Tade, *1993 External Debt Bulletin* and *Treasury Monthly Indicators.*

Table N. **Central government budget**

TL billion

	1986	1987	1988	1989	1990	1991	1992	1993
Revenue	7 154	10 445	17 587	31 369	56 573	96 747	174 224	351 392
Tax revenue	5 972	9 051	14 232	25 550	45 399	78 643	141 602	264 273
Non-tax revenue	1 182	1 394	3 355	5 819	11 174	18 104	32 622	87 119
Expenditure	8 560	13 044	21 447	38 871	68 527	130 263	221 658	485 249
Current personnel expenditure	1 840	2 996	5 053	12 539	26 465	49 291	94 076	169 511
Other current expenditure	1 211	1 542	2 407	4 121	6 987	11 112	20 145	35 318
Investment	2 019	2 642	3 564	5 818	10 055	17 146	29 239	53 161
Transfers	3 490	5 864	10 423	16 393	25 020	52 714	78 198	227 259
of which: SEEs	138	446	1 025	1 223	1 265	12 191	8 145	25 850
Interest payment	1 331	2 266	4 978	8 259	13 966	24 073	40 298	116 470
Budget balance	-1 406	-2 599	-3 860	-7 502	-11 954	-33 516	-47 434	-133 857
Deferred payments	227	911	36	38	1 161	3 555	-778	10 905
Advance payments	-424	-878	-117	-677	-1 561	-3 465	-11 227	-3 151
Cash balance	-1 603	-2 566	-3 941	-8 141	-12 354	-33 426	-59 439	-126 103
Borrowing	2 027	2 976	6 347	12 376	18 012	22 399	55 375	110 960
Domestic	1 269	2 045	3 816	8 983	12 523	11 510	35 657	64 820
Foreign	758	931	2 531	3 393	5 489	10 889	19 718	46 140
Repayments	-1 557	-2 346	-3 738	-6 798	-10 029	-18 199	-35 929	-59 763
Domestic	-793	-1 149	-1 383	-3 001	-4 581	-9 231	-20 249	-34 685
Foreign	-764	-1 197	-2 355	-3 797	-5 448	-8 968	-15 680	-25 078
Short-term borrowing (net)	925	1 268	1 064	1 452	2 263	23 509	41 372	75 251
Central Bank	257	355	675	457	331	10 719	17 394	53 010
Treasury bills	668	913	389	995	1 932	12 790	23 978	22 241
Other borrowing [1]	208	668	268	1 111	2 108	5 718	-1 380	-345

1. Including errors and omissions and change in cash/bank.
Source: Undersecretariat of Treasury and Foreign Trade, *Treasury Monthly Indicators.*

Table O. **Central government budget revenue**

New classification[1]

TL billion

	1986	1987	1988	1989	1990	1991	1992	1993
Taxes on income	3 053	4 425	6 919	13 469	23 246	40 419	70 134	125 793
Personal income tax	2 104	3 093	4 801	9 871	18 609	33 356	60 056	106 661
Corporate income tax	949	1 332	2 118	3 598	4 637	7 063	10 078	19 132
Taxes on wealth	53	68	147	177	411	675	1 259	2 531
Motor vehicles tax	43	51	121	134	329	539	1 020	2 078
Inheritance and gift tax	10	17	26	43	82	137	239	453
Taxes on goods and services	1 853	2 768	4 487	7 639	13 667	24 673	47 341	89 447
Domestic value-added tax (VAT)	1 040	1 563	2 661	4 176	7 650	14 541	27 053	50 892
Supplementary VAT (monopoly products)	178	264	288	461	372	605	187	388
Petroleum consumption tax	54	71	159	656	1 224	2 370	6 769	12 791
Motor vehicles purchase tax	43	74	127	214	585	981	2 378	5 322
Banking and insurance tax	94	155	374	643	1 164	2 119	3 922	7 129
Stamp duty	250	379	534	876	1 497	2 457	4 153	7 971
Fees	194	262	344	613	1 176	1 600	2 879	4 954
Taxes on foreign trade	993	1 777	2 672	4 245	8 057	12 864	22 848	46 213
Customs duty[2]	292	431	600	724	1 063	1 036	1 725	13 171
VAT on imports	528	1 004	1 517	2 285	4 721	8 291	15 034	30 985
Other foreign trade taxes	173	342	555	1 236	2 273	3 537	6 089	2 057
Abolished taxes	20	13	7	18	18	7	20	289
Total tax revenue	5 972	9 051	14 232	25 548	45 399	78 638	141 602	264 273
Non-tax regular revenue	502	809	1 353	2 439	4 267	3 926	7 649	17 636
Corporate profits and State shares	33	45	63	111	206	318	536	526
Revenues of State property[3]	69	110	245	454	1 828	869	1 367	4 535
Interest and claims	59	88	109	348	246	267	404	1 223
Fines	111	165	328	522	698	853	2 533	3 410
Other revenue	230	401	608	1 004	1 289	1 619	2 809	7 942
Special revenue and funds[4]	156	34	1 228	1 950	4 909	13 230	23 593	66 126
Total non-tax revenue	658	843	2 581	4 389	9 176	17 156	31 242	83 762
Annex budget revenue	128	206	351	440	663	953	1 380	3 357
Total consolidated budget revenue	6 758	10 100	17 164	30 377	55 238	96 747	174 224	351 392

1. With the introduction of value-added tax (VAT) in January 1985, the following taxes were abolished: sales, communications and advertisement tax, production tax, production tax on petroleum and monopoly products.
2. Including customs duty on petroleum.
3. In 1990 and in 1991, privatisations revenues are included.
4. From 1992 onwards, transfers from Extra-budgetary Funds are included.
Source: Ministry of Finance and Customs.

BASIC STATISTICS

STATISTIQUES DE BASE :

COMPARAISONS INTERNATIONALES

	Units	Reference period [1]	Australia	Austria
Population				
Total	Thousands	1992	17 489	7 884
Inhabitants per sq. km	Number	1992	2	94
Net average annual increase over previous 10 years	%	1992	1.4	0.4
Employment				
Civilian employment (CE)[2]	Thousands	1992	7 637	3 546
Of which: Agriculture	% of CE		5.3	7.1
Industry	% of CE		23.8	35.6
Services	% of CE		71	57.4
Gross domestic product (GDP)				
At current prices and current exchange rates	Bill. US$	1992	296.6	186.2
Per capita	US$		16 959	23 616
At current prices using current PPPs[3]	Bill. US$	1992	294.5	142
Per capita	US$		16 800	18 017
Average annual volume growth over previous 5 years	%	1992	2	3.4
Gross fixed capital formation (GFCF)	% of GDP	1992	19.7	25
Of which: Machinery and equipment	% of GDP		9.3	9.9
Residential construction	% of GDP		5.1	5.7
Average annual volume growth over previous 5 years	%	1992	−1	5.1
Gross saving ratio[4]	% of GDP	1992	15.6	25.1
General government				
Current expenditure on goods and services	% of GDP	1992	18.5	18.4
Current disbursements[5]	% of GDP	1992	36.9	46.2
Current receipts	% of GDP	1992	33.1	48.3
Net official development assistance	% of GNP	1992	0.33	0.3
Indicators of living standards				
Private consumption per capita using current PPPs[3]	US$	1992	10 527	9 951
Passenger cars, per 1 000 inhabitants	Number	1990	430	382
Telephones, per 1 000 inhabitants	Number	1990	448	589
Television sets, per 1 000 inhabitants	Number	1989	484	475
Doctors, per 1 000 inhabitants	Number	1991	2	2.1
Infant mortality per 1 000 live births	Number	1991	7.1	7.4
Wages and prices (average annual increase over previous 5 years)				
Wages (earnings or rates according to availability)	%	1992	5	5.4
Consumer prices	%	1992	5.2	3
Foreign trade				
Exports of goods, fob*	Mill. US$	1992	42 844	44 361
As % of GDP	%		14.4	23.8
Average annual increase over previous 5 years	%		10.1	10.4
Imports of goods, cif*	Mill. US$	1992	40 751	54 038
As % of GDP	%		13.7	29
Average annual increase over previous 5 years	%		8.6	10.7
Total official reserves[6]	Mill. SDRs	1992	8 152	9 006
As ratio of average monthly imports of goods	Ratio		2.4	2

* At current prices and exchange rates.
1. Unless otherwise stated.
2. According to the definitions used in OECD *Labour Force Statistics.*
3. PPPs = Purchasing Power Parities.
4. Gross saving = Gross national disposable income minus private and government consumption.
5. Current disbursements = Current expenditure on goods and services plus current transfers and payments of property income.
6. Gold included in reserves is valued at 35 SDRs per ounce. End of year.
7. Including Luxembourg.

BASIC STATISTICS: INTERNATIONAL COMPARISONS

...gium	Canada	Denmark	Finland	France	Germany	Greece	Iceland	Ireland	Italy	Japan	Luxembourg	Mexico	Netherlands	New Zealand	Norway	Portugal	Spain	Sweden	Switzerland	Turkey	United Kingdom	United States
0 045	28 436	5 171	5 042	57 374	80 569	10 300	260	3 547	56 859	124 320	390	89 540	15 184	3 443	4 287	9 858	39 085	8 668	6 875	58 400	57 998	255 610
329	3	120	15	105	226	78	3	50	189	329	150	45	372	13	13	107	77	19	166	75	237	27
0.2	1.5	0.1	0.4	0.5	2.7	0.5	1.1	0.2	0	0	0.6	2.1	0.6	0.8	0.4	0	0.3	0.4	0.6	2.2	0.3	1
3 724	12 240	2 613	2 163	22 032	28 708	3 634 (91)	140 (91)	1 113 (91)	21 271	64 360	162 (91)	23 403 (90)	6 576	1 467	1 970	4 498	12 359	4 195	3 481	18 600	25 175	117 598
2.6	4.4	5.2	8.6	5.2	3.1	22.2 (91)	10.7 (91)	13.8 (91)	8.2	6.4	3.7 (91)	22.6 (90)	4	10.8	5.6	11.6	10.1	3.3	5.6	43.9	2.2	2.9
27.7	22.7	27.4	27.9	28.9	38.3	27.5 (91)	26.4 (91)	28.9 (91)	32.2	34.6	31.5 (91)	27.8 (90)	24.6	22.6	23.5	33.2	32.4	26.5	33.9	22.1	26.5	24.6
69.7	73	68.7	63.5	65.9	58.5	50.2 (91)	62.9 (91)	57.2 (91)	59.6	59	64.8 (91)	49.6 (90)	71.4	66.6	71	55.3	57.5	70.2	60.6	34	71.3	72.5
220.9	563.7	141.6	106.4	1 322.1	1 801.3	77.9	6.9	51	1 220.6	3 662.5	10.6	329.3	320.2	41.1	113.1	84.2	576.3	247.2	240.9	159.1	1 042.8	5 937.3
21 991	19 823	27 383	21 100	23 043	27 770	7 562	26 595	14 385	21 468	29 460	27 073	3 678	21 089	11 938	26 386	8 541	14 745	28 522	35 041	2 724	17 981	23 228
181.5	536.8	91.2	73.2	1 063.7	1 328.2	85.1	4.4	45.3	1 005.9	2 437.2	8.5	493.1	257.2	49.2	75.7	95.9	500.2	143.3	152.8	297.3	941.1	5 953.3
8 071	19 585	17 628	14 510	18 540	20 482	8 267	17 062	12 763	17 373	19 604	21 833	5 507	16 942	14 294	17 664	9 743	12 797	16 526	22 221	5 019	16 227	23 291
3.1	1.1	1.1	-0.1	2.4	4	2.2	-0.1	5.6	2.2	4.2	4.1	3.1	3	0.4	1.3	3.3	3.3	0.6	1.7	3.7	0.9	1.9
19.1	18.8	15.1	18.5	20	20.9	18	17.5	15.9	19.1	30.8	27.7	20.8	20.3	16.4	19.2	26.2	21.8	17	23.7	23	15.6	15.6
8.6	6.2	6.8	6.8	8.8	9.2	7.9	5.3	6.7	8.9	12.4	..	10.6	9.4	8.2	..	..	6.8	6.2	8	8.5	7.2	7.2
4.6	6.4	3	4.6	5.1	6.1	3.8	4.8	4.3	5.3	5.2	..	4.5	5	4.1	..	..	4.3	5.9	15.7[10]	7.6	3	3.7
7.1	1.4	-4.2	-4.3	3.3	5	4.9	-3	2.9	2.7	6.5	6.5	8.9	2.5	-1.3	-5.4	6.8	6.2	-0.6	1.5	4.6	0.6	0.7
21.3	12.8	18	12.1	19.8	22.1	15.5	14.3	18.5	17.2	33.9	60.2	16.1	23.5	19.2	21	25.3	19.1	14.1	29.7	23.1	12.8	14.5
14.7	21.9	25.5	24.9	18.8	17.9	19.7	20.2	16.1	17.6	9.3	17.1	10.1 [9]	14.5	16.3	22.4	18.3	17	27.8	14.3	12.9	22.3	17.7
54.6	49.2	58.2	56.1	48.4	44.1	47.1	32.1	..	51.5	25.9	..	..	55.3	..	..	..	..	64.6	35.1	..	42.1	36.7
49.7	43.7	57.3	53.2	46.1	45	39.9	34.8	..	43.6	34	..	..	54.1	..	..	..	..	59.6	34.7	..	38	31.6
0.39	0.45	0.98	0.61	0.63	0.42	..	..	0.14	0.34	0.3	0.34	..	0.86	0.24	1.13	0.36	0.26	1	0.47	..	0.31	0.2
420	11 863	9 120	8 285	11 144	11 186	5 929	10 557	7 443	10 936	11 191	12 285	3 978	10 213	8 769	9 189	6 124	8 083	8 907	13 043	3 206	10 397	15 637
387	469	311	386	413	480	169	464	228	478	282	470	85	356	440	378	260	307	418	441	29	361	568
546	570	972	530	482	671	458	496	279	555	421	413	118	462	430	502	263	323	681	905	151	434	509
447	626	528	488	400	506	195	319	271	423	610	252	127	485	372	423	176	389	471	406	174	434	814
3.6	2.2	2.8	2.5	2.7	3.2	3.4	2.8	1.5	1.3	1.6	2.1	1.1	2.5	1.9	3.1	2.8	3.9	2.9	3	0.9	1.4	2.3
8.4	6.8	7.5	5.8	7.3	7.1	9	5.5	8.2	8.3	4.6	9.2	43	6.5	8.3	7	10.8	7.8	6.1	6.2	56.5	7.4	8.9
4.1	4.4	4.7	7	3.9	5.1	17.7	..	5.1	6.9	4	..	5.3	2.7	3.9	5	..	7.7	7.3	..	..	8.3	2.9
2.7	4.2	3.3	5	3.1	2.8	16.6	14.3	3.2	5.9	2.2	3	35.8	2.1	4.3	4.2	11.2	6	6.8	4.1	66.6	6.3	4.3
3 264 [7]	134 696	39 732	23 956	235 911	429 727	9 541	1 571	28 297	178 217	339 553	..[8]	46 196	140 234	9 831	35 140	17 990	64 509	55 980	65 478	14 853	190 103	448 033
55.8	23.9	28.1	22.5	17.8	23.9	12.2	22.7	55.5	14.6	9.3	..	14	43.8	23.9	31.1	21.4	11.2	22.6	27.2	9.3	18.2	7.5
8.2	7.4	9.2	4.3	9.8	7.9	6.2	3	12.1	8.9	8.1	..	17.7	8.6	6.5	10.4	14.5	13.7	4.8	7.5	7.5	7.8	12
6 133 [7]	122 445	33 707	21 166	230 050	408 180	23 012	1 710	22 467	188 524	233 100	..	62 129	134 578	9 159	26 057	29 588	99 659	49 916	65 587	23 267	220 994	531 070
56.6	21.7	23.8	19.9	17.4	22.7	29.5	24.7	44	15.4	6.4	..	18.9	42	22.3	23	35.1	17.3	20.2	27.2	14.6	21.2	8.9
8.4	6.9	8.4	2.4	8.5	12.4	10.7	1.6	10.5	8.6	9.2	..	36.1	8.1	4.8	2.9	17.4	15.3	4.2	5.3	10	7.5	5.5
0 037 [7]	8 314	8 032	3 792	19 657	66 158	3 486	362	2 502	20 104	52 089	..	13 776	15 954	2 239	8 684	13 912	33 094	16 454	24 185	4 480	26 648	43 831
1	0.8	2.9	2.1	1	1.9	1.8	2.5	1.3	1.3	2.7	..	2.7	1.4	2.9	4	5.6	4	4	4.4	2.3	1.4	1

. Included in figures for Belgium.
. Refers to the public sector including public enterprises.
. Including non-residential construction.

Sources: Population and Employment: OECD, Labour Force Statistics. GDP, GFCF, and General Government: OECD, National Accounts, Vol. I. Indicators of living standards: Miscellaneous national publications. Wages and Prices: OECD, Main Economic Indicators. Foreign trade: OECD, Monthly Foreign Trade Statistics, series A. Total official reserves: IMF, International Financial Statistics.

November 1994

EMPLOYMENT OPPORTUNITIES

Economics Department, OECD

The Economics Department of the OECD offers challenging and rewarding opportunities to economists interested in applied policy analysis in an international environment. The Department's concerns extend across the entire field of economic policy analysis, both macroeconomic and microeconomic. Its main task is to provide, for discussion by committees of senior officials from Member countries, documents and papers dealing with current policy concerns. Within this programme of work, three major responsibilities are:

- to prepare regular surveys of the economies of individual Member countries;
- to issue full twice-yearly reviews of the economic situation and prospects of the OECD countries in the context of world economic trends;
- to analyse specific policy issues in a medium-term context for the OECD as a whole, and to a lesser extent for the non-OECD countries.

The documents prepared for these purposes, together with much of the Department's other economic work, appear in published form in the *OECD Economic Outlook, OECD Economic Surveys, OECD Economic Studies* and the Department's *Working Papers* series.

The Department maintains a world econometric model, INTERLINK, which plays an important role in the preparation of the policy analyses and twice-yearly projections. The availability of extensive cross-country data bases and good computer resources facilitates comparative empirical analysis, much of which is incorporated into the model.

The Department is made up of about 80 professional economists from a variety of backgrounds and Member countries. Most projects are carried out by small teams and last from four to eighteen months. Within the Department, ideas and points of view are widely discussed; there is a lively professional interchange, and all professional staff have the opportunity to contribute actively to the programme of work.

Skills the Economics Department is looking for:

a) Solid competence in using the tools of both microeconomic and macroeconomic theory to answer policy questions. Experience indicates that this normally requires the equivalent of a Ph.D. in economics or substantial relevant professional experience to compensate for a lower degree.

b) Solid knowledge of economic statistics and quantitative methods; this includes how to identify data, estimate structural relationships, apply basic techniques of time series analysis, and test hypotheses. It is essential to be able to interpret results sensibly in an economic policy context.

c) A keen interest in and extensive knowledge of policy issues, economic developments and their political/social contexts.

d) Interest and experience in analysing questions posed by policy-makers and presenting the results to them effectively and judiciously. Thus, work experience in government agencies or policy research institutions is an advantage.

e) The ability to write clearly, effectively, and to the point. The OECD is a bilingual organisation with French and English as the official languages. Candidates must have excellent knowledge of one of these languages, and some knowledge of the other. Knowledge of other languages might also be an advantage for certain posts.

f) For some posts, expertise in a particular area may be important, but a successful candidate is expected to be able to work on a broader range of topics relevant to the work of the Department. Thus, except in rare cases, the Department does not recruit narrow specialists.

g) The Department works on a tight time schedule with strict deadlines. Moreover, much of the work in the Department is carried out in small groups. Thus, the ability to work with other economists from a variety of cultural and professional backgrounds, to supervise junior staff, and to produce work on time is important.

General information

The salary for recruits depends on educational and professional background. Positions carry a basic salary from FF 305 700 or FF 377 208 for Administrators (economists) and from FF 438 348 for Principal Administrators (senior economists). This may be supplemented by expatriation and/or family allowances, depending on nationality, residence and family situation. Initial appointments are for a fixed term of two to three years.

Vacancies are open to candidates from OECD Member countries. The Organisation seeks to maintain an appropriate balance between female and male staff and among nationals from Member countries.

For further information on employment opportunities in the Economics Department, contact:

Administrative Unit
Economics Department
OECD
2, rue André-Pascal
75775 PARIS CEDEX 16
FRANCE

E-Mail: compte.esadmin@oecd.org

Applications citing "ECSUR", together with a detailed *curriculum vitae* in English or French, should be sent to the Head of Personnel at the above address.

MAIN SALES OUTLETS OF OECD PUBLICATIONS
PRINCIPAUX POINTS DE VENTE DES PUBLICATIONS DE L'OCDE

ARGENTINA – ARGENTINE
Carlos Hirsch S.R.L.
Galería Güemes, Florida 165, 4° Piso
1333 Buenos Aires   Tel. (1) 331.1787 y 331.2391
Telefax: (1) 331.1787

AUSTRALIA – AUSTRALIE
D.A. Information Services
648 Whitehorse Road, P.O.B 163
Mitcham, Victoria 3132   Tel. (03) 873.4411
Telefax: (03) 873.5679

AUSTRIA – AUTRICHE
Gerold & Co.
Graben 31
Wien I   Tel. (0222) 533.50.14

BELGIUM – BELGIQUE
Jean De Lannoy
Avenue du Roi 202
B-1060 Bruxelles   Tel. (02) 538.51.69/538.08.41
Telefax: (02) 538.08.41

CANADA
Renouf Publishing Company Ltd.
1294 Algoma Road
Ottawa, ON K1B 3W8   Tel. (613) 741.4333
Telefax: (613) 741.5439
Stores:
61 Sparks Street
Ottawa, ON K1P 5R1   Tel. (613) 238.8985
211 Yonge Street
Toronto, ON M5B 1M4   Tel. (416) 363.3171
Telefax: (416)363.59.63
Les Éditions La Liberté Inc.
3020 Chemin Sainte-Foy
Sainte-Foy, PQ G1X 3V6   Tel. (418) 658.3763
Telefax: (418) 658.3763

Federal Publications Inc.
165 University Avenue, Suite 701
Toronto, ON M5H 3B8   Tel. (416) 860.1611
Telefax: (416) 860.1608
Les Publications Fédérales
1185 Université
Montréal, QC H3B 3A7   Tel. (514) 954.1633
Telefax : (514) 954.1635

CHINA – CHINE
China National Publications Import
Export Corporation (CNPIEC)
16 Gongti E. Road, Chaoyang District
P.O. Box 88 or 50
Beijing 100704 PR   Tel. (01) 506.6688
Telefax: (01) 506.3101

CZECH REPUBLIC – RÉPUBLIQUE TCHÈQUE
Artia Pegas Press Ltd.
Narodni Trida 25
POB 825
111 21 Praha 1   Tel. 26.65.68
Telefax: 26.20.81

DENMARK – DANEMARK
Munksgaard Book and Subscription Service
35, Nørre Søgade, P.O. Box 2148
DK-1016 København K   Tel. (33) 12.85.70
Telefax: (33) 12.93.87

EGYPT – ÉGYPTE
Middle East Observer
41 Sherif Street
Cairo   Tel. 392.6919
Telefax: 360-6804

FINLAND – FINLANDE
Akateeminen Kirjakauppa
Keskuskatu 1, P.O. Box 128
00100 Helsinki
Subscription Services/Agence d'abonnements :
P.O. Box 23
00371 Helsinki   Tel. (358 0) 12141
Telefax: (358 0) 121.4450

FRANCE
OECD/OCDE
Mail Orders/Commandes par correspondance:
2, rue André-Pascal
75775 Paris Cedex 16   Tel. (33-1) 45.24.82.00
Telefax: (33-1) 49.10.42.76
Telex: 640048 OCDE
Orders via Minitel, France only/
Commandes par Minitel, France exclusivement :
36 15 OCDE
OECD Bookshop/Librairie de l'OCDE :
33, rue Octave-Feuillet
75016 Paris   Tel. (33-1) 45.24.81.67
(33-1) 45.24.81.81
Documentation Française
29, quai Voltaire
75007 Paris   Tel. 40.15.70.00
Gibert Jeune (Droit-Économie)
6, place Saint-Michel
75006 Paris   Tel. 43.25.91.19
Librairie du Commerce International
10, avenue d'Iéna
75016 Paris   Tel. 40.73.34.60
Librairie Dunod
Université Paris-Dauphine
Place du Maréchal de Lattre de Tassigny
75016 Paris   Tel. (1) 44.05.40.13
Librairie Lavoisier
11, rue Lavoisier
75008 Paris   Tel. 42.65.39.95
Librairie L.G.D.J. - Montchrestien
20, rue Soufflot
75005 Paris   Tel. 46.33.89.85
Librairie des Sciences Politiques
30, rue Saint-Guillaume
75007 Paris   Tel. 45.48.36.02
P.U.F.
49, boulevard Saint-Michel
75005 Paris   Tel. 43.25.83.40
Librairie de l'Université
12a, rue Nazareth
13100 Aix-en-Provence   Tel. (16) 42.26.18.08
Documentation Française
165, rue Garibaldi
69003 Lyon   Tel. (16) 78.63.32.23
Librairie Decitre
29, place Bellecour
69002 Lyon   Tel. (16) 72.40.54.54

GERMANY – ALLEMAGNE
OECD Publications and Information Centre
August-Bebel-Allee 6
D-53175 Bonn   Tel. (0228) 959.120
Telefax: (0228) 959.12.17

GREECE – GRÈCE
Librairie Kauffmann
Mavrokordatou 9
106 78 Athens   Tel. (01) 32.55.321
Telefax: (01) 36.33.967

HONG-KONG
Swindon Book Co. Ltd.
13-15 Lock Road
Kowloon, Hong Kong   Tel. 2376.2062
Telefax: 2376.0685

HUNGARY – HONGRIE
Euro Info Service
Margitsziget, Európa Ház
1138 Budapest   Tel. (1) 111.62.16
Telefax : (1) 111.60.61

ICELAND – ISLANDE
Mál Mog Menning
Laugavegi 18, Pósthólf 392
121 Reykjavik   Tel. 162.35.23

INDIA – INDE
Oxford Book and Stationery Co.
Scindia House
New Delhi 110001   Tel.(11) 331.5896/5308
Telefax: (11) 332.5993
17 Park Street
Calcutta 700016   Tel. 240832

INDONESIA – INDONÉSIE
Pdii-Lipi
P.O. Box 4298
Jakarta 12042   Tel. (21) 573.34.67
Telefax: (21) 573.34.67

IRELAND – IRLANDE
Government Supplies Agency
Publications Section
4/5 Harcourt Road
Dublin 2   Tel. 661.31.11
Telefax: 478.06.45

ISRAEL
Praedicta
5 Shatner Street
P.O. Box 34030
Jerusalem 91430   Tel. (2) 52.84.90/1/2
Telefax: (2) 52.84.93
R.O.Y.
P.O. Box 13056
Tel Aviv 61130   Tél. (3) 49.61.08
Telefax (3) 544.60.39

ITALY – ITALIE
Libreria Commissionaria Sansoni
Via Duca di Calabria 1/1
50125 Firenze   Tel. (055) 64.54.15
Telefax: (055) 64.12.57
Via Bartolini 29
20155 Milano   Tel. (02) 36.50.83
Editrice e Libreria Herder
Piazza Montecitorio 120
00186 Roma   Tel. 679.46.28
Telefax: 678.47.51
Libreria Hoepli
Via Hoepli 5
20121 Milano   Tel. (02) 86.54.46
Telefax: (02) 805.28.86
Libreria Scientifica
Dott. Lucio de Biasio 'Aeiou'
Via Coronelli, 6
20146 Milano   Tel. (02) 48.95.45.52
Telefax: (02) 48.95.45.48

JAPAN – JAPON
OECD Publications and Information Centre
Landic Akasaka Building
2-3-4 Akasaka, Minato-ku
Tokyo 107   Tel. (81.3) 3586.2016
Telefax: (81.3) 3584.7929

KOREA – CORÉE
Kyobo Book Centre Co. Ltd.
P.O. Box 1658, Kwang Hwa Moon
Seoul   Tel. 730.78.91
Telefax: 735.00.30

MALAYSIA – MALAISIE
University of Malaya Bookshop
University of Malaya
P.O. Box 1127, Jalan Pantai Baru
59700 Kuala Lumpur
Malaysia   Tel. 756.5000/756.5425
Telefax: 756.3246

MEXICO – MEXIQUE
Revistas y Periodicos Internacionales S.A. de C.V.
Florencia 57 - 1004
Mexico, D.F. 06600   Tel. 207.81.00
Telefax: 208.39.79